VOLUME THREE

Imperial Japanese Navy *vs* The Allies
New Guinea & the Solomons 1942–1944

MICHAEL JOHN CLARINGBOULD

Avonmore Books

Pacific Adversaries Volume Three
Imperial Japanese Navy vs The Allies New Guinea & the Solomons 1942-1944

Michael John Claringbould
ISBN: 978-0-6486659-5-3

First published 2020 by Avonmore Books
Avonmore Books
PO Box 217
Kent Town
South Australia 5071
Australia
Phone: (61 8) 8431 9780
www.avonmorebooks.com.au

A catalogue record for this
book is available from the
National Library of Australia

Cover design & layout by Diane Bricknell

Front Cover Caption: Ensign Frederick Streig claims a Zero over Rabaul on 27 January 1944. His VF-17 F4U-1A Corsair squadron #3 unusually retained the red surround on the stars and bars, mostly painted out on the squadron's other fighters.

Rear cover Caption: A late Model 52 shotaicho Zero, discernible by its protruding exhaust stacks, cruises over Rabaul in late January 1944. This fighter carries "Rabaul Air Force" markings, using a tail coding system still not fully understood to this day.

Errata for Pacific Adversaries Volume 2:
p.62: the P-40N illustrated has November 1943 markings which does not align with the January 1943 incident discussed in Chapter 9.
Back cover: the date in the caption is January 1943. It should read October 1943.

Contents

The author in Darwin with the Japanese military attaché to Australia, 17 February 2017.

About the Author

Michael Claringbould – Author & Illustrator

Michael spent his formative years in Papua New Guinea in the 1960s, during which he became fascinated by the many WWII aircraft wrecks which lay around the country. Over subsequent decades he assisted identifying such aircraft and helped the US and Japanese governments recover missing aircraft crews in New Guinea and the Solomons.

Michael has served widely overseas as an Australian diplomat, including in the South Pacific where he had the fortune to return to Papua New Guinea for three years commencing in 2003.

Michael was a contributing editor for *Flightpath* magazine and has written several books on the Pacific War. More recently, his history of the Tainan Naval Air Group in New Guinea, *Eagles of the Southern Sky*, received worldwide acclaim as the first English-language history of any Japanese air unit. An executive member of Pacific Air War History Associates, Michael also holds an Australian pilot license and a PG4 paraglider rating. These days he also enjoys developing his skills as a digital 3D aviation artist.

Other Books by the Author

Black Sunday (2000)

Eagles of the Southern Skies (with Luca Ruffato, 2012)

Operation I-Go Yamamoto's Last Offensive – New Guinea and the Solomons April 1943 (Avonmore Books, 2020)

P-39 / P-400 Airacobra versus A6M2/3 Zero-sen New Guinea 1942 (Osprey, 2018)

P-47D Thunderbolt versus Ki-43 Hayabusa New Guinea 1943/44 (Osprey, 2020)

Pacific Adversaries Volume One: Japanese Army Air Force vs The Allies New Guinea 1942-1944 (Avonmore Books, 2019)

Pacific Adversaries Volume Two: Imperial Japanese Navy vs The Allies New Guinea & the Solomons 1942-1944 (Avonmore Books, 2020)

Pacific Profiles Volume One Japanese Army Fighters New Guinea & the Solomons 1942-1944 (Avonmore Books, 2020)

South Pacific Air War Volume 1: The Fall of Rabaul December 1941–March 1942 (with Peter Ingman, Avonmore Books, 2017)

South Pacific Air War Volume 2: The Struggle for Moresby March–April 1942 (with Peter Ingman, Avonmore Books, 2018)

South Pacific Air War Volume 3: Coral Sea & Aftermath May–June 1942 (with Peter Ingman, Avonmore Books, 2019)

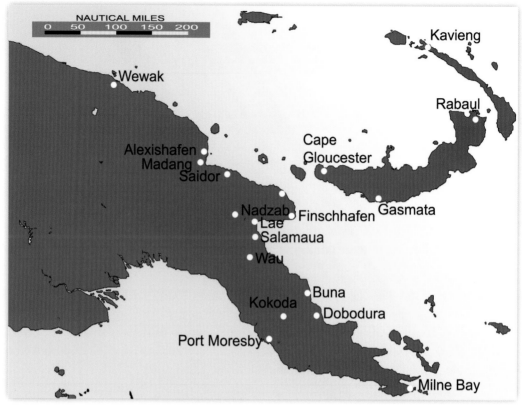

Key locations in New Guinea featured in the text.

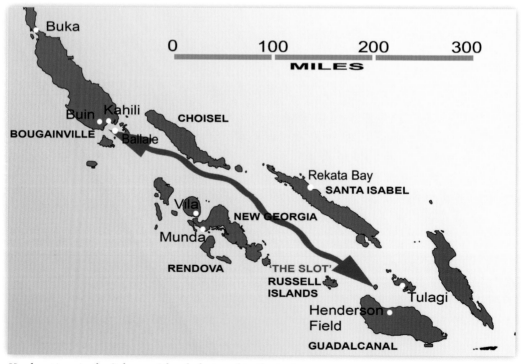

Key locations in the Solomon Islands featured in the text.

Introduction

This volume is the third in the *Pacific Adversaries* series which relates detailed stories of aerial warfare in the South Pacific by aligning combatants. Each account has been chosen because the relevant Japanese and Allied records accurately match. Often the actual outcomes are at odds to the exaggerated claims made by both sides upon which most traditional histories have relied to date. Photographic, technical and other evidence enables accurate profiles to be created from each encounter. Japanese records including operations records never before accessed by Western authors are consulted extensively.

Through these chosen snapshots, the *Pacific Adversaries* series portrays the South Pacific conflict as accurately as possible. This third volume focuses exclusively on Allied confrontations with the Japanese Naval Air Force (JNAF) in New Guinea and the Solomons, known to the Japanese as the "South Seas".

The JNAF operated from ships, carriers and land bases with an eclectic inventory of fighters, bombers, flying boats, floatplanes and reconnaissance aircraft. These deployed widely with distinct and dissimilar doctrine, command structures and aircraft designs compared to their army counterparts. Yet, precious few accurate narratives of JNAF operations appear in the English language. The rich and colourful history of the JNAF is more curious than the associated falsehoods and myths which continue to persist.

The JNAF first appeared in the South Pacific in December 1941 and was at the vanguard of offensive efforts during the course of 1942. Following the bloody Guadalcanal campaign, the JNAF fought a largely defensive war in New Guinea and the Solomons against increasingly powerful Allied forces. Perhaps surprisingly, right through to the end of 1943 the JNAF offered significant resistance to the Allies and refused to concede air superiority in the vicinity of its key base of Rabaul. Only in 1944, when units were withdrawn to the Central Pacific and the Philippines, was the JNAF presence in the South Pacific finally wound down to just a token force.

Never before have such snapshots matched adversaries so meticulously, from which the reader will draw their own assessments. I hope you enjoy these narratives which shine light on key events in Pacific skies so many years ago.

Michael John Claringbould
Canberra
April 2020

Pacific Adversaries Volume Three– Glossary and Abbreviations

Japanese terms are in italics. All Japanese names are presented in the traditional way of writing Japanese, with the surname presented first.

AA	Anti-Aircraft
AK	Cargo Ship, auxiliary (USN)
ASI	Air Speed Indicator
AT	Ocean-going Tug (USN)
BG	Bombardment Group (USAAF)
BS	Bombardment Squadron (USAAF)
Bu. No.	Bureau Number (USN)
Buntai	Equivalent to a *chutai* but usually accompanied by administrative or established command status.
Buntaicho	Leader of a *buntai*
CA	Heavy cruiser (USN)
Chutai	Japanese aircraft formation normally comprised of nine aircraft.
Chutaicho	Flight leader of a *chutai*.
CINCPAC	Commander-in-Chief, US Pacific Fleet (USN)
CN	Constructor's Number
CO	Commanding Officer
DD	Destroyer (USN)
FG	Fighter Group (USAAF)
FS	Fighter Squadron (USAAF)
FCPO	Flying Chief Petty Officer
FPO1c	Flying Petty Officer First Class
FPO2c	Flying Petty Officer Second Class
Hikocho	Administrative commander of a *Kokutai*, senior to the *Hikotaicho* (operational commander).
Hikotaicho	commander of a *kokutai*
Hokoku	Inscriptions (translating as "patriotic") which signified that an aircraft was donated by an individual, organisation or corporation. The donor's name appeared in the *kanji* subscript.
HQ	Headquarters
IJN	Imperial Japanese Navy
JAAF	Japanese Army Air Force
JNAF	Japanese Naval Air Force
Kokutai	An IJN air group, consisting of between three and six *chutai*.

CHAPTER 1
The Big Splash

The Lockheed Lightning proved highly suited to Pacific service – eventually accounting for many hundreds of American claimed kills. However, the very first claim was perhaps the most unusual, with the victory not from gunfire but from the splash of a 500-pound bomb dropped in the ocean.

Following arrival of the first F-4 reconnaissance versions of the Lockheed Lightning in Australia in April 1942, the first combat version of the new type only began arriving five months later in September 1942. Although some sixty of the long-awaited type had been delivered to Amberley, Queensland, by the following month, none were assigned to forward units straight away. A litany of problems delayed their entry into service including leaking fuel tanks, overheating superchargers, engine coolant problems, intermittent invertors and temperamental armament solenoids. All of these problems required tinkering. Some were solved by field modifications, and others by assiduous tuning and adjustment. A complicating factor was that aircraft engineers in New Guinea's combat units had until now only dealt with more elementary machines such as Airacobras and Warhawks. The Lightning was an exponential step-up in complexity.

The initial and most serious challenge was leaking fuel tanks caused by manufacturing defects. A main lower panel had to be removed from the wing under-surface to permit access to the fuel cell. Screws had to first be removed around the filler neck inside the cell before it could be removed. To gain sufficient leverage to remove the screws engineers had to enter the cell to shoulder height and then work quickly as the fumes could make them sick. Groundcrew kept a flashlight handy to regularly inspect the inside of all cells.

Furthermore, when compared with existing fighter types in the SWPA the Lightning's routine maintenance workload was about four times as much. The extra engine incurred some of the extra effort, but it was mainly the more complex systems which added time especially the hydraulics. However, the extra effort was readily accepted, since the Lightning was recognised as a potent new weapon which could gain a significant advantage over the enemy.

The first combat Lightings were P-38F models assigned to the USAAF 39th FS, commanded by veteran pilot Major George Prentice who had fought Zeros over Darwin with the 49th FG. The Lightning allegedly scored its very first kill in a most unorthodox way. Exceptionally, rather than a fighter sweep, the first planned mission was a night dive-bombing attack on a convoy bringing reinforcements to Buna in late November 1942. Accordingly, eight 500-pound bombs, one per aircraft, were delivered to Schwimmer 'drome, Port Moresby, to do the job. The pilots were incredulous as none had dive-bombing experience, nor had they trained for night-time attacks. Fortunately, the mission was cancelled at the last minute when it was determined that the target ships had already unloaded their cargoes and turned around.

Lieutenant Charles King, on the wing of his P-38F, who participated in the Lae mission and thought the original night attack plan was "insane".

Another Lae mission participant was Lieutenant John "Shady" Lane seen in the cockpit of his P-38F at Schwimmer 'drome.

Instead the pilots were ordered to dump the bombs on Lae's runway the next morning, 26 November 1942. Five Lightnings departed to do the job, led by recently promoted Captain Bob Faurot. In the new fast and heavy fighter, he overshot the target and his bomb exploded in the sea just off the end of Lae's runway. A massive geyser rose from the detonation just as a Zero was taking off.

The Americans mistook the departing Zeros below as efforts to intercept them, however it was instead the first of twelve launching to escort four Vals on a mission to attack Allied troop positions around Dobodura. One Zero flew straight into the geyser and some Americans thought that the blast flipped it into the sea. The Lightnings pulled away from the target straight ahead, then banked starboard at full power to get home quickly and avoid the Zeros. These eyewitness pilots vouched confirmation to Faurot's submission for one Japanese fighter to be awarded as a "kill".

The paperwork for Faurot's claim soon arrived at the desk of the commander of the Fifth Air Force, General George Kenney. Instead of approving the request, Kenney confronted Faurot as to whether he had the nerve to claim it as the first P-38 kill in the SWPA. A beaming Faurot responded by asking whether he would also receive the Air Medal. Kenney responded that he wanted Zeros shot down and not simply splashed. In the event Faurot was not awarded the kill even though the alleged victory continued to be celebrated within the squadron.

There is no doubt that the geyser erupted close to the departing fighter, but regrettably for the Americans it did not bring it down as claimed. Zeros from both Nos. 582 and 252 *Ku* were stationed at Lae that morning, and six Zeros from each unit combined forces to escort the four

Warrant Officer Tsunoda Kazuo who led the combined Zero contingent on 26 November 1942 from Lae.

One of the first P-38Fs to arrive in New Guinea is inspected at Schwimmer 'drome in late 1943.

No. 582 *Ku* Vals. Warrant Officer Tsunoda Kazuo led the Zero contingent which had started launching at 0815 when Faurot's Lightnings dove across Lae at low level. The Vals and Zeros then headed to Dobodura.

Later at 0900 the Zeros fought off 8th FS Warhawks in half an hour of combat around Dobodura in several combat actions which included strafing Allied positions. All Japanese aircraft had returned safely to Lae by 1035 save one Zero lost. This was No. 582 *Ku* pilot Superior Airman Tatsuo Nobuhito who was shot down around 0920 by one of the Warhawks which were (wrongly) awarded three aerial victories. However no Zero was lost to Faurot's Lightnings and in fact their brief appearance is not mentioned in the operations log of either of the Japanese units involved.

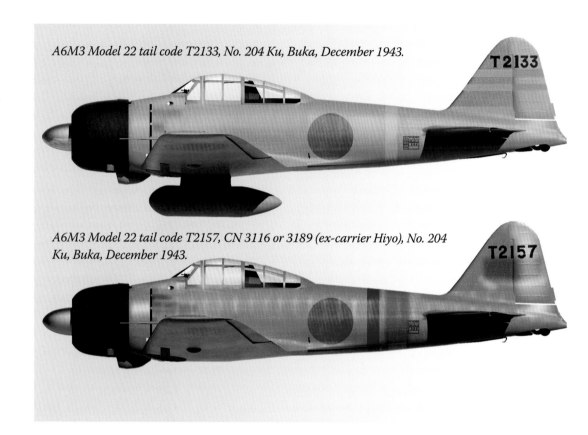

A6M3 Model 22 tail code T2133, No. 204 Ku, Buka, December 1943.

A6M3 Model 22 tail code T2157, CN 3116 or 3189 (ex-carrier Hiyo), No. 204 Ku, Buka, December 1943.

CHAPTER 2
Luckiest Men in the Pacific

During a surprise encounter with a Flying Fortress, Superior Airman Sugita Shoichi pressed his attack so close into the underside of the great bomber that he collided with it. Two extraordinary tales of survival followed.

Beyond any doubt the two luckiest airmen in the Pacific on 1 December 1942 were Fortress tail gunner Corporal Joseph Hartman and Zero pilot Superior Airman Sugita Shoichi. Extreme misadventure resulted in these two becoming miracle survivors of a chance mid-air collision. Hartman subsequently spent 67 days in tropical isolation before he returned to Guadalcanal. During his recovery he painstakingly documented the incident, from which we know precisely what happened on that fateful day. Although Hartman's tail gunner position permitted only a rear view, he could hear his comrades' radio chatter through his headphones. For nine of the ten Fortress crew however, it was their final journey. Aside from details in the relevant unit log, the Japanese perspective is provided via the memoirs of the No. 204 *Ku buntaicho*, Lieutenant Kofukuda Mitsugu.

The Fortress in which Hartman flew was named *Omar Khayyam* in honour of the Persian philosopher born in 1048 AD. Its arrival in theatre was somewhat errant. First assigned to Lieutenant Edwin McAnelly and crew, they launched from Hamilton Field for a Pacific crossing to Australia on 5 September 1942. However, they were instead assigned at Plaine des Gaiacs airfield in New Caledonia to serve with the 11th Bombardment Group. After a furtive conference among themselves, and having anticipated female company in Australia, the crew snuck a take-off the next day on a pretext of checking their compass. They flew directly to Eagle Farm airfield in Brisbane instead, thence the next day to Charters Towers, where *Omar Khayyam's* crew was welcomed by the 43rd BG, Fifth Air Force, which was their original assigned unit.

A subsequent series of robust telegraphic messages from New Caledonia soon followed them, however, and they were ordered back. Upon return to the French outpost, *Omar Khayyam* was reassigned to the 431st BS and flown onwards to Guadalcanal. For the Americans there in late 1942 it was still a dark time on the island, where the Japanese had yet to be dislodged. Several major Japanese pushes had threatened Henderson Field itself, and a major US ground campaign was in the making to eliminate Japanese Army units holed up in the hills behind the field. Complemented by night-time artillery and aircraft bombardments, life for Americans based on "The 'Canal" was hard. Whilst most Fortress missions from there were bombing ones, they also conducted aerial supply drops to US troops. Solo shipping searches and weather reconnaissance missions to remote northern sectors were also on the cards.

Against this grim backdrop, on 1 December 1942 *Omar Khayyam* was tasked to conduct a lone search and photographic mission to Bougainville, some 350 miles distant. On the way the crew would also reconnoiter the Japanese airfield being built at Munda, New Georgia. Departure was planned early at 0530, and *Omar Khayyam* headed out on time and climbed to 17,000 feet. The crew was aware that the mission might not be a routine milk run. Only recently, on 18 November 1942, their Commanding Officer "Blondie" Saunders had been shot down in the area by fierce and persistent Japanese fighters. Despite being rescued after ditching his Fortress, the incident underlined the real threat of lurking danger.

It was relatively cold at cruise altitude, around four degrees Celsius, and the crew was accordingly clad in leather flying gear. The bomber photographed the southern end of Bougainville, then banked for home. Enemy interception which had been anticipated materialised in the shape of six Zeros, which rose to greet the lone bomber from the island airfield of Ballale. A brief and inconsequential aerial battle ensued at 1000 from which the side gunners claimed two Zeros. The B-17 continued on its easterly course to the north end of Choisel Island where, still at the same altitude, it was intercepted by another flight of Zeros. These circled and maneuvered around and out of range of the Fortress, initially reluctant to press their attack, when suddenly the crew's attention was directed to a lone fighter. Its appearance startled them as the Zero broke downwards through cloud before lunging upwards directly towards the Fortress.

Curiously, the Americans wrongly thought this Zero dropped four aerial bombs, which they judged fell well short. Then before evasive action could be taken the oncoming fighter collided with them. A combined collision speed in excess of 400 knots from underneath tore through the bomber's fuselage just behind the wings. The Fortress broke cleanly in two, the forward portion bursting into flames and flat-spinning its nine occupants to oblivion. Meanwhile the tail section carrying Hartman rolled cleanly to one side and fell in a stable configuration.

The responsible Zero pilot was Superior Airman Sugita Shoichi of No. 204 *Ku* who had teamed

A line-up of No. 204 Ku Model 21 Zeros at Kahili in mid-1943 after receiving field camouflage.

Boeing B-17E SPOOK-KI of the 11th BG about to start up at Henderson Field, Guadalcanal in late 1942.

up that morning with two contemporary pilots of identical rank, *shotaicho* Kanda Saji and Hitomi Kiju, not for combat but for training purposes. There had been much discussion among the unit's pilots at Buin on how best to bring down a Fortress. They had concluded that a head-on attack from slightly below was the best method, concentrating fire into what they considered the airframe's weakest area - where the wing joined the fuselage.

That morning the unit had broken into two flights. The first, comprising two *shotai* totaling four Zeros led by Lieutenant Shibuya Kiyohara, would pose as a Fortress, whilst the second flight of Sugita, Kanda and Hitomi would practice head-on attacks. Shibuya climbed his flight away from Ballale early at 0450 to first conduct a patrol. The four returned to Ballale at 0820 and refueled, departing again at 1000 in a wide gentle climbing turn over Ballale. Shibuya became concerned when Kanda's *shotai* failed to show, however Kanda's *shotai* were a long way from Ballale. When Kanda sighted *Omar Khayyam* in the distance he gestured to Hitomi and Sugita in the direction of the Fortress and off they went.

Sugita initially kept his distance before lining himself up. He intended firing his 20mm cannons into the Fortress' belly, in which he estimated he had a half second window of opportunity. Sugita later related that when he fired at the looming Fortress it suddenly felt like a collapsing roof upon him. He instinctively ducked in his seat, and by the time his tail fin collided with his quarry he was unsure whether or not his cannon had struck home. Remarkably, Kanda remained in control of his Zero and could barely contain his joy as he witnessed the main section of the Fortress spiraling out of control. He was soon on the ground after a gingerly descent. As he taxied in it was glaringly obvious that nearly half his fin had been torn off by the collision. Rather than being jubilant, Sugita looked contrite and pensive as he climbed out of his fighter. Bringing down a Fortress was one thing, however a mid-air collision was against the rules.

Buntaicho Lieutenant Kofukuda Mitsugi was there to greet him and rather than admonishing Sugita he congratulated him. Even though there had been a collision it was with an enemy aircraft, and the Fortress had been destroyed. Later that evening Kofukuda presented Sugita with a bottle of sake. The next morning Kofukuda assembled all No. 204 *Ku* pilots and underlined that they should get in as close as possible, firing when almost upon the bomber. Kofukuda stressed that the normal method of placing an aircraft in the sights at a distance would not work against a Fortress, and accordingly he urged his pilots to follow Sugita's uncompromising close-in example, although short of actual collision.

Meanwhile, the impact of Sugita's Zero knocked Hartman senseless. When he regained consciousness shortly afterwards he saw the gaping hole where the rest of the bomber had been. He wrenched open the starboard escape hatch just forward of the tail-plane to assess his situation. The tail section in which he was now the only passenger had rolled on one side yet was stably falling towards the ocean below. Judging that there was still enough altitude to safely jump, he grabbed his parachute but quickly discovered that the girth of his heavy winter flying suit allowed no time to connect the leg straps, and with only seconds to impact there was no time to make adjustments. He fastened only the chest strap, hoping it would hold, and then clawed his way back to the hatch. His first attempt to exit failed as the air pressure threw him back inside. Using more force, Hartman made a desperate exit on the second attempt, hoping he would not be slammed against the horizontal stabiliser as he exited. As soon as he lunged clear he jerked the ripcord, but a violent opening at high speed placed concentrated strain on his chest strap, causing him to pass out for a second time. Hartman estimated he had bailed out at about 2,000 feet. Incredibly, he regained consciousness just in time to slip out of his chest harness a few feet above the water.

Hartman dropped into a quiet swell about 150 metres from a tropical shoreline. He estimated that he came ashore about fifteen miles south east of the northern end of Choisel. When he collapsed on the beach he discovered to his amazement that he had unconsciously removed all his clothes sometime during his swim to shore. It was in this exposed condition that he was greeted about half an hour later by two islanders who had seen his descent and found him on the beach pondering his next move. Hartman would spend 67 days hiding from the Japanese with assistance from these locals before he was finally rescued by an Australian coastwatcher and returned to his unit. A grateful Hartman was subsequently granted extended leave in Auckland, New Zealand.

Against all odds Hartman survived where nine others had not. The tail should have spun out of control, thus restraining him inside with G forces, but its stable descent allowed him to exit. Only one parachute chest strap had restrained him. He lost consciousness twice, yet regained sufficient composure to open the chute and slip from the harness just above the water before it likely would have drowned him. Finally, Hartman successfully evaded capture in an area dominated by Japanese forces. Hartman's saga is truly a unique and epic episode of the Pacific War, however arguably Sugita was almost as lucky. Surviving a mid-air collision is unlikely in

Bitch Kitty was another 11th BG B-17E to serve with the 11th BG at Guadalcanal.

itself. Furthermore, had the fin been completely removed it is almost certain the resultant G force would have pinned him in the cockpit, just as it had restrained most of the Fortress crew.

Born in Nigita prefecture, Sugita survived this remarkable day to go on to become a high-scoring pilot. Later he was one of the six pilots selected to escort Admiral Yamamoto Isoroku on 18 April 1943 when the Admiral was shot down over southern Bougainville. Sugita was subsequently shot down and killed by a USN pilot on 15 April 1945.

Notes on No. 204 *Ku* markings

This unit underwent two distinct markings phases. The first was when it replaced the previous No. 6 *Ku* tail codes with an unhyphenated black tail code beginning with prefix T2, as reflected in both profiles here. Around March 1943, or possibly earlier, No. 204 *Ku* started applying green camouflage in the field and switched the format of the tail code into a two-level system in white letters, the T2 prefix centered above the three-digit identifier. At least two different colours were used for tail bands throughout, however the unit regularly operated in three-*chutai* structures and in addition to red and yellow it is likely there was a third colour, unknown at this stage. *Chutaicho* were indicated by a double fuselage band, and *shotaicho* by tail bands.

B-17E Yankee Doodle flown by future creator of the TV series Star Trek, Gene Roddenberry. Standing are an unidentified pilot (left) and crew chief Sergeant Roy Davenport.

CHAPTER 3
Confused Identity

A hastily conceived New Year's Eve "booze run" flight resulted in the crash of a Flying Fortress on Espiritu Santo. For decades this wreck has been confused with that of an almost identically named Fortress on Guadalcanal.

It was 31 December 1942 and New Year's Eve celebrations were in full swing at "Buttons" – the codename for Espiritu Santo in the New Hebrides – but early that evening it became clear in the 431ˢᵗ BS officers club that they would soon run out of liquor. Many patrons had commenced celebrating early and robust discussion quickly followed as to where more liquor might be sourced. The problem was that on New Year's Eve quality liquor was at a premium and difficult to obtain anywhere on Santo. However, there were bombers on hand so discussion arose as to which nearby Pacific bases might have some. No-one was sure that liquor would be available at Efate, only an hour's flying time south, while the more distant bases of Plaine des Gaiacs and Tontouta on New Caledonia were ruled out as both airfields were a long way from the capital Noumea, which was the most likely liquor source

The 431ˢᵗ BS of the 11ᵗʰ BG was operating the B-17E Flying Fortress and had arrived at Espiritu Santo from Hawaii via Nadi, Fiji, in mid July 1942. During their brief Fiji stay the peaceful sight of workers in cane fields and colourfully dressed Fijian policemen had left an impression on the transiting crews. It was also recalled that not only was Nadi airfield close to PX outlets, but the USN also had a well-stocked PBY base nearby at Lautoka. Despite the formidable distance of just over three and a half hours flying time to get there, pilot Lieutenant Robert Andrews from Wisconsin, aged 24, accompanied by Squadron Commanding Officer Captain Jack Levy, aged 25, boarded the bomber. Although both were inebriated, Andrews would fly the bomber with Levy as his co-pilot. It was hoped that Levy's more senior rank would assist in securing suitable liquor stocks in Fiji. Levy and Andrews had both previously seen combat at Midway in June 1942.

Back at the officer's club, the 431ˢᵗ BS pilots felt they had much to celebrate. Shortly after Midway the 11ᵗʰ BG had been categorised as a mobile unit by the Joint Command Staff in response to a USN Navy request for reconnaissance aircraft to assist in locating Japanese shipping. It was felt that the armed Fortress had sufficient firepower to deter Japanese fighters while undertaking such long-range duties. The group arrived at Buttons on 22 July 1942 where it soon became part of the Thirteenth Air Force. Their task evolved into also attacking Japanese positions and airfields, and to do this they would often stage through Henderson Field on Guadalcanal.

Meanwhile in the darkness at 2030, Andrews had barely warmed up the engines of *Yankee Doodle Jr* before roaring down Bomber Field #1. Underlining their ambitious logistics plan drawn up at short notice was the fact that, optimistically allowing only an hour to successfully secure liquor at the other end, they would not return to Buttons until around 0430 the next morning.

The wreckage of Yankee Doodle just after it crashed on the morning of 2 August 1943 on Guadalcanal with the future Star Trek creator at the controls.

Yankee Doodle Jr being bombed up on Espiritu Santo in the New Hebrides.

When Andrews lifted off *Yankee Doodle Jr* he climbed the Fortress steeply then banked starboard for a reverse heading for Fiji. The bomber stalled and fell over on one wing, crashing into jungle just beyond a maintenance encampment inhabited by their fellow 42nd BS. The Fortress dove into the ground, exploded and then caught fire, destroying most of the forward section and wings. Levy was killed instantly in the crash and Andrews was badly injured with critically burned and broken limbs. Despite the best medical treatment available on the island at the nearby military hospital he finally succumbed to his wounds two days later. Fortuitously the Fortress did not crash into one of several nearby ammunition dumps which had appeared all over the island.

Until now post-war accounts wrongly state that *Yankee Doodle Jr* crashed offshore Espiritu Santo close to the airfield. This historical inaccuracy led to decades of post-war confusion in correctly identifying the Fortress wreckage which still lies in jungle north of the former Bomber Field #1 and is visited occasionally as a remote tourist attraction.

The wreckage instead has often been misidentified over the years as that of another B-17E ironically sharing the namesake *Yankee Doodle* (without the "*Jr*") which crashed on take-off from

Guadalcanal at dawn on 2 August 1943. This was flown by Lieutenant Gene Roddenberry who found his Fortress couldn't attain sufficient airspeed to get airborne on take-off. He aborted power but ran into coconut palms at the end of the runway. The crash wiped out the bomber, save for the tail, and it was completely consumed by flames. Roddenberry was exonerated from any blame, with the accident judged to have been caused by mechanical failure. He went on to become a successful screen writer, his most famous creation being the television series *Star Trek*.

The wreckage of Yankee Doodle Jr was hauled to a nearby aircraft dump where it lies today.

Espiritu Santo hosted three large bomber fields, this is Bomber #3. Note the many ships in the channel adjacent to the airfield.

One of the many ammunition dumps which existed on Espiritu Santo throughout the Pacific war.

Map of the Shortlands base used by R-Area Force floatplanes and flying boats. There were three separate operational, administrative and engineering areas, all connected by regular launch services.

Lieutenant-Commander Ikekami Satoru's Emily overhead Espiritu Santo around midnight on 20 January 1943.

CHAPTER 4
Emily versus Bessie

In early 1943 an Emily flying boat departed its Solomons base on a long-range mission that would be the only Japanese attack ever mounted against the New Hebrides. While the flying boat commander claimed to have destroyed a military base on Espiritu Santo, the only casualty was a cow named Bessie.

Following the appearance of the first Kawanishi H8K1 Emily flying boat in Rabaul Harbour in March 1942, No. 14 *Ku* had sent four to Rabaul in mid-July 1942 to bomb Townsville. The Toko *Ku*, a unit formed and based in the port of Tokyo, was the next unit to arrive at Rabaul with a handful of Emilys. These were initially used for long-range sector patrols.

The huge aircraft sometimes required replacements in the form of essential parts which were not immediately available, resulting in downtime. In addition, the airframe was powered by a unique engine model from Mitsubishi's successful Kasei series which consumed a unique oil specification. These early Toko *Ku* detachments therefore needed to bring sufficient oil reserves to keep the big flying boats airworthy until more stocks could be shipped from Japan. In the 1 November 1942 IJN restructure, Toko *Ku* was redesignated No. 851 *Ku*, by which time its forward base had become the Shortland Islands.

The base was where Rear Admiral Jojima Takatsugu, commander of the 11th Seaplane Tender Division was based with his forward-deployed floatplanes, known as the R-Area Force. Only five miles south of the IJN airfield on the island of Ballale, the anchorages around the Shortland Islands were almost perfect for seaplane operations, which ranged from single-engine floatplanes all the way up to the large four-engine Emily flying boats. Japanese planners had been aware of the area's potential from pre-war intelligence. Protected from prevailing winds and with unobstructed deep channels for seaplane operations, three proximate islands housed a diversified complex. Floatplanes were anchored off Shortland Island itself, while a hundred metres across the channel, a substantial accommodation complex had been built on Faisi. This was the first island in the Solomons Islands occupied by Japanese, which they did in the early hours of 30 March 1942 when two Special Naval Landing Force platoons captured it unopposed. By early 1943 workshop and support facilities had been built on Bambagiai Island just across the narrow southern channel, and a regular launch service plied between the islands in the vicinity, and often up to Ballale too. Anti-aircraft gun positions were scattered throughout the complex and on the surrounding hills.

The support cadre for No. 851 *Ku* became well-ensconced on Faisi with about three hundred technicians and aircrew based there. The unit's Emilys ran almost daily shuttles to Rabaul on flights just short of three hours duration. The voluminous aircraft were loaded at Malaguna Bay near Rabaul with whatever was required for the island base. Two Emilys went missing consecutively on evening patrols down The Slot on 13 and 14 November, with aggressive

This heavy anti-aircraft battery overlooking Second Channel on Espiritu Santo was photographed on 14 January 1943, just six days before the raid.

B-17s correctly assumed as being the chief suspect. Many of these patrols were very long-range and of up to twelve hours duration. On Christmas Day 1942, a pair of Emilys conducted a ten-minute running fight with an 11th BG B-17 at dawn, with one of the giants sustaining ten hits.

Lieutenant-Commander Ikekami Satoru commanded No. 851 *Ku*'s operations at the Shortland's base as *hikotaicho*. He often visited Rabaul to deal with administrative minutiae but also spent much time on Faisi. Cognisant of an Allied build-up of shipping and air power at Espiritu Santo, the commander of the 11th Fleet, Vice Admiral Kusaka Jinichi, authorised Ikekami to conduct a one-off strike against the expanding US Naval base there. This was considerable distance of 850 miles from the Shortlands and it was decided that a solo Emily would conduct a "night attack" mission. Ikekami decided the mission sufficiently important that he would command it himself, although he was accompanied by another Lieutenant-Commander whose position is unspecified, making up a total crew for the flying boat of thirteen.

A PBM Mariner flying boat on finals for a water landing descends over the USS Tangier just west of Luganville, Espiritu Santo, on the afternoon of the raid on 20 January 1943.

On the afternoon of 20 January 1943, sixteen 60-kilogram bombs were slung underneath the Emily's wings, eight per pylon secured between the inner and outer engines. Pilot Warrant Officer (surname undecipherable) Akio and co-pilot FPO1c Hiramatsu Misuo alighted the Emily from Shortland Harbour at 1735 and arrived overhead Espiritu Santo at exactly midnight. There they loitered for forty-five minutes leading the Americans below to think there were several aircraft involved. At 0045 the Emily logged:

Reconnaissance and bombing mission completed. Destroyed the military base and left four fires burning.

The resultant CINCPAC summary records that:

On the night of 20/21 January small groups of enemy planes bombed Espiritu Santo but caused no damage.

In fact, five of the Emily's bombs exploded on the USN repair and oil storage facility at Aore Island just across Second Channel from Espiritu Santo, killing a plantation cow named Bessie. The demise of this grazing innocent was the only casualty of the raid.

The harbour below had been, in fact, full of warships comprising TF67. These were anchored throughout the channel and included the cruisers *Nashville*, *Honolulu*, *Helene* and *St Louis* together with the destroyers *Drayton*, *Lamson*, *Perkins* and *Reid*. Nonetheless the ineffectual raid raised eyebrows with Washington, as Secretary of the Navy Frank Knox was visiting Espiritu on an inspection tour when Ikekami's flying boat made its uninvited appearance.

Knox flew to Guadalcanal the next day to continue his tour where two night raids against the big island made the USN brass wonder whether or not the Japanese had broken their communications codes and were targeting Knox. This was not the case, it was simply that Knox' visit coincided with these Japanese initiatives. On 24 January Knox proceeded to Suva, Fiji, thus completing his inspection of forward Pacific bases. His final duty before returning back to the US mainland was to award two medals at an evening ceremony held on the veranda of the British governor's residence there. This curious solo raid marked the first and last time any Japanese aircraft raided the New Hebrides.

The Emily's target: the port of Luganville

Aircrew board a moored Emily for a night mission. Note the bombs slung between the two port engines.

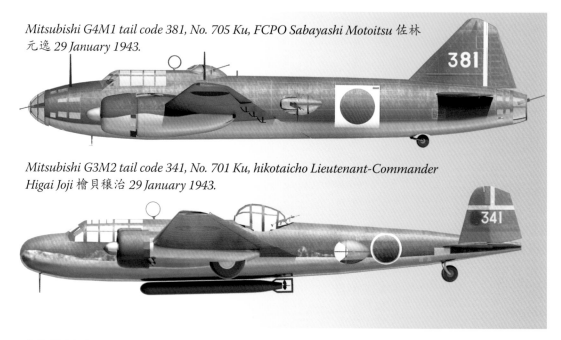

Mitsubishi G4M1 tail code 381, No. 705 Ku, FCPO Sabayashi Motoitsu 佐林 元逸 29 January 1943.

Mitsubishi G3M2 tail code 341, No. 701 Ku, hikotaicho Lieutenant-Commander Higai Joji 檜貝穣治 29 January 1943.

Lieutenant-Commander Higai Joji leads No. 701 Ku away from Rabaul in mid-afternoon overcast.

CHAPTER 5
Higai's Demise

Leading a force of antiquated Nells, veteran IJN aviator Lieutenant-Commander Higai Joji skilfully executes a night torpedo strike against a USN convoy. The cruiser USS Chicago is seriously damaged, but Higai's Nell is one of two downed by AA fire.

The heavy cruiser USS *Chicago* was lost to a series of aerial torpedo strikes during 29-30 January 1943 while operating as part of TF18 south of Guadalcanal. During the first attack she was hit twice in rapid succession, then also the next day whilst under tow by four more torpedoes. In spite of extensive flooding from the first two hits, *Chicago* would likely have survived the first round, however the additional torpedoes from the second attack were more than the ship could absorb.

Commander of TF18 was Rear Admiral Richard Giffen who, although new to the Pacific theatre, was considered experienced from time spent on Atlantic and North African operations. Despite the threat of Japanese bombers for two days, Giffen remained steadfast in making a pre-ordained rendezvous with four destroyers off Cape Hunter at 2100 on the evening of the first attack. Once achieved, TF18 would then guard The Slot to ward off possible Japanese warships that might interfere with a US troop convoy scheduled to return combat-weary soldiers to New Zealand for some well-earned rest.

Back at Rabaul, Vice Admiral Kusaka Jinichi had different concerns of which the Americans were unaware. He also had to remove troops from Guadalcanal however his objective was a safe and permanent evacuation from Guadalcanal termed Operation KE. Long-range reconnaissance flights had determined that US ships in the vicinity threatened KE. That mid-afternoon Kusaka thus authorised a strike force of 32 Japanese bombers, broken into two equal contributions by Nos. 701 and 705 *Ku*. Launching from Vunakanau at 1435 were 16 No. 705 *Ku* Bettys led by Lieutenant-Commander Nakabayashi Tomo'o, followed by 16 No. 701 *Ku* G3M2 Nells ten minutes later, led by *hikotaicho* Lieutenant-Commander Higai Joji. An old hand who enjoyed a fine reputation in the land attack corps, Higai had previously served as *hikotaicho* with the Kasumigaura *Ku* from 1 September 1941, a unit steeped in IJN tradition.

Although No. 701 *Ku* was equipped with antiquated Nell bombers from the China era, Higai had enthusiastically adapted his crews to night attack and they had since invested much time in honing their art. One Nell from his starboard *chutai* of four aborted after take-off, leaving the rest to continue southeast alongside their Betty counterparts. Both units were eager to try out their new suite of night attack skills, which included the use of "pathfinder" aircraft. Their task was to bracket the nautical targets with lights before commencing an attack: white flares were first laid as illuminating footlights, complemented by methodically spaced red and green flares on either side. The pathfinders could then, by discerning the interval a ship took to sail between the lights, calculate and convey vital information including speed, composition and direction. To undertake the pathfinder tasks for this mission, two Nells had left Vunakanau previously at 1342, led by Lieutenant Wakana Asao. Meanwhile a solitary Betty (tail code #381) would act as a snooper for the No. 705 *Ku* Bettys. This departed ten minutes before the main No. 705 *Ku* attack force and was flown by FCPO Sabayashi Motoitsu with an extra observer aboard. Sabayashi would successfully mark TF18 then return safely to Vunakanau at 0020 the next morning.

Whilst the Japanese bomber strike force headed for TF18, just before midday an unidentified aircraft bothered American radar screens. This was the second of two No. 851 *Ku* H8K1 Emily flying boats, the first of which had launched from the Shortlands before dawn at 0517. The intruder on the radar screen included crewmember *hikotaicho* Commander Ide Masaru seated in the chief observer's seat behind the pilot. At 1109 Ide's crew located TF18 in Japanese search sector A2. Ide radioed Rabaul the position of the American ships, then loitered at a distance, before returning to the Shortlands at 1400. Escorting carriers scrambled Wildcats to try and find the snooper, but heavy overcast deterred any sightings. Radio silence was maintained by the ships for security reasons, meaning the Wildcats could not be vectored. Nonetheless, there is a curious entry in the Emily's log indicating tail gunner FPO2c Futai (first name undecipherable) fired six rounds of 20mm ammunition. Did Futai see a fighter in the murk or was he simply test-firing his cannon?

Sunset found TF18 zigzagging at 24 knots to the northeast in approach formation. Giffen's flagship, the cruiser *Wichita* was among cruisers which steamed in two columns some 2,500 yards apart: *Montpelier, Cleveland* and *Columbia* to port, with *Wichita, Chicago* and *Louisville* to starboard. Six destroyers formed a protective semicircle some two miles ahead. Whilst such grouping was efficient for anti-submarine purposes, it left aft beams and quarters exposed to aerial attack.

After sunset, worried radar operators aboard the flagship watched as radar spots grew in size and closed in. Both the Nells and Bettys in separate groups circled astern of their quarry in one of Nakabayashi's signature moves - to benefit from the blackness of the eastern atmosphere. At 1920 his sixteen No. 705 *Ku* Bettys commenced a long run-in. About four minutes later, right on the end of twilight, destroyer *Waller* (DD-466) on the starboard flank commenced firing on the incoming bombers. Immediately thereafter *Chicago* also opened fire with her 40mm starboard

The location of the two torpedo hits on USS Chicago made by No. 701 Ku at dusk on 29 January 1943.

Mitsubishi G4M1 tail code 379, CN 463, Hokoku 1006, was a No. 705 Ku participant on the 29 January 1943 mission.

battery followed by the 5-inch ones, using full radar control. Arcs of AA reached out from both cruiser columns. One Betty splashed astern of *Chicago*, between her and *Waller*, leaving a pool of flaming petrol where pilot FCPO Imabayashi Monzaburo and seven other Betty aircrew had perished. During the attack a crewmember aboard another Betty was killed by American gunfire.

None of TF18's ships sustained damage, although a loud clang against *Louisville's* hull betrayed a dud torpedo. Rear Admiral Richard Giffen, apparently undistracted by the failed Betty attack, remained determined to make the rendezvous and altered neither TF18's speed nor heading. In fact, when the Bettys had barely cleared the area he ordered TF18 to abandon their zigzag course to save time. This facilitated the job-at-hand for Higai's fifteen loitering No. 701 *Ku* Nells. These had arrived in the target area commensurate with Nakabayashi's Bettys and had meanwhile lurked in the darkness. Keen observers aboard the Nells could see through binoculars that TF18 maintained its steady course and were determined to attack.

A No. 701 Ku G3M2 Nell prepares for a mission from Vunakanau. Note the bomb racks bolted to the fuselage underbelly.

A No. 701 Ku G3M2 Nell brackets a Model 11 Betty taxiing at Vunakanau in early 1943.

As per IJN custom, Lieutenant-Commander Higai Joji led the first *chutai* in, commencing his attack run at 1933. His six Nells raced low towards the target, giving themselves considerable distance from the looming ships to steady the approach. Defending fire from tracers and shell bursts illuminated the night sky with the 5-inch guns being the brightest offenders. These were so bright that one ship's report complains that the flashes limited observations. Some American observers submitted incorrectly that the attackers were Type 97s, a JAAF bomber with codename Sally. Vivid flames suddenly lit up an incoming Nell as reported by *Chicago*:

> The bomber was hit repeatedly and exploded close aboard on the port bow. The flames from this plane were very brilliant, and as it was now completely dark undoubtedly silhouetted *Chicago* for the planes which followed.

The Japanese log this loss at 1942 as that of the Nell commanded by FCPO Tageki Tsuyoshi and his crew of seven (Japanese and American logs differ by two minutes throughout most of the engagement). Then Higai's Nell was also splashed by American guns in a similar manner three minutes later. A valued veteran of the IJN land attack corps was lost, and the two shoot-downs left thirteen Nells seeking safe haven in the dark. A main cluster of ten Nells found each other for the return journey and made Vunakanau at 0015 early next morning. Three more Nells

A G3M2 Nell attracts curious locals at Kavieng.

were stragglers which had been hit by gunfire from the defending US ships. These put down on Bougainville bases for precautionary landings where they overnighted. FPO1c Fukuda Seiji was the first to make landfall, putting into Buin at 2220, followed by two more which landed at Buka at 2310 and 2330 (FPO2c Sano Tadasaku and FPO1c Isumi Atsuo respectively). Their crews grabbed what little sleep they could, then pre-flighted the bombers at sunrise next morning. Determining all were safe to fly, all three were back at Vunakanau around 0900.

Meanwhile *Chicago* had logged a torpedo hitting her starboard side at 1940, followed two minutes later by a second. Together they halted *Chicago*, which was noted by observers as falling out of formation at 1948. A third torpedo had hit Giffen's flagship, the *Wichita*, but luckily for the admiral it failed to explode. Aboard *Chicago* the first torpedo struck aft of the engine room, and the second close to No.3 fire room. The explosions stopped the rotation of all four shafts, directional control was lost, and the rudder jammed ten degrees port. Flooding extended throughout the amidships section, comprising about one-third the length of the vessel. A starboard list quickly developed to eleven degrees, and when the ship settled by the stern, steam pressure was lost. Leaks were plugged and weakened bulkheads shored. Normal power failed due to the flooding, but diesel generators quickly energised the emergency power circuits. The list was soon checked at 11 degrees, and further settling was arrested with eight feet of freeboard at the stern. By about 0100 the next morning sufficient fuel oil had been transferred from the starboard to port fuel tanks to rebalance the ship.

To try and remain hidden, Giffen had forbade his ship's gunners from firing without confirmed targets. In the event USN radar screens plotted another solitary Japanese lurking in the area until 2335, clearly trying to monitor Giffen's movements. This was another No. 851 *Ku* H8K1 Emily flying boat from the Shortlands which in fact did so successfully. Proof as to how seriously Rabaul viewed the presence of the American warships is demonstrated by the fact that it was commanded (and flown) by flag officer Commander Kobata Hiro'o. His Emily found Giffen's ships around 1830, loitered at a distance, then turned for home at 2348, thirteen minutes after he faded from US radar screens. Kobata safely alighted back in Shortlands Harbor at 0215, with Rabaul fully updated of Giffen's movements.

Meanwhile shortly after midnight *Chicago* was taken under tow by the *Louisville* (CA-28). Once the cruiser was underway her rudder slid into neutral by opening the hydraulic steering valves, and the rudder was then locked. At 0800 on 30 January the fleet tug USS *Navajo* (AT-64) took over the tow. Giffen ordered that *Chicago* be towed to the New Hebrides where she could receive temporary repairs. However, in this vulnerable state *Chicago* was torpedoed again the next day and sunk.

This No. 701 Ku Nell, tail code 325, was captured at Lae in September 1943.

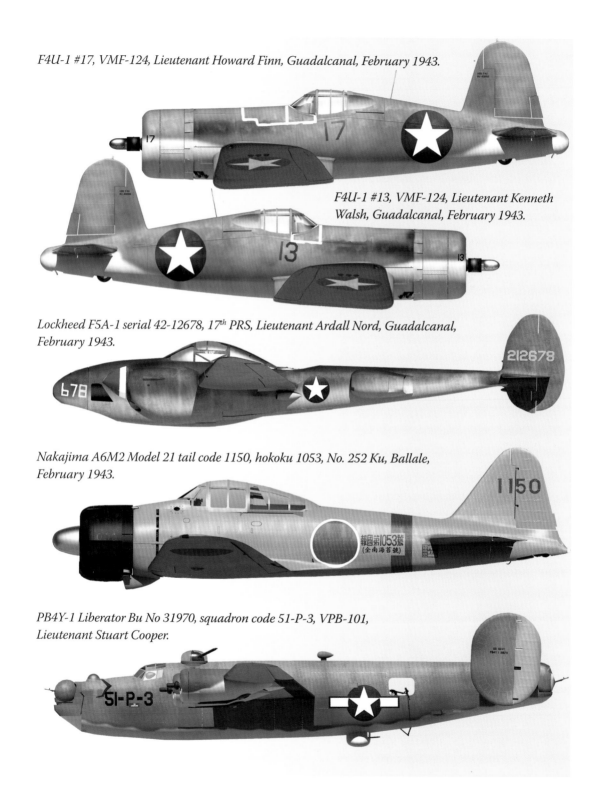

F4U-1 #17, VMF-124, Lieutenant Howard Finn, Guadalcanal, February 1943.

F4U-1 #13, VMF-124, Lieutenant Kenneth Walsh, Guadalcanal, February 1943.

Lockheed F5A-1 serial 42-12678, 17th PRS, Lieutenant Ardall Nord, Guadalcanal, February 1943.

Nakajima A6M2 Model 21 tail code 1150, hokoku 1053, No. 252 Ku, Ballale, February 1943.

PB4Y-1 Liberator Bu No 31970, squadron code 51-P-3, VPB-101, Lieutenant Stuart Cooper.

CHAPTER 6
Saint Valentine's Day Massacre

On 14 February 1943 a combination of Zeros and Rufe floatplanes won a convincing victory against newly arrived Lightning and Corsair fighters. To the Americans, who lost nine aircraft including two Liberators, the engagement became known as the Saint Valentine's Day Massacre and forced a cessation of daylight missions over the southern Bougainville area.

Both the Lockheed Lightning and Vought F4U Corsair eventually proved to be superior fighters in the Pacific, however their introduction to the theatre demonstrated some of their weaknesses. Neither became superb fighters until both their pilots and leadership structures worked out how to deploy them effectively. Optimum circumstances for effective engagement did not always occur, and the Zero remained successful against these high-performance fighters throughout 1943 to a greater degree than is often portrayed. Essentially, this translated into a contest of speed and altitude for the Americans, versus the Zero's outstanding agility and range.

The Corsair's first worldwide combat engagement, escorting Liberators on a shipping strike, unfolded on 14 February 1943 and became known as the "Valentine's Day Massacre" due to the high American losses. The first Corsairs had only arrived in theatre two days previously when they had conducted patrols and familiarisation flights. Prior to the strike a 17th PRS F-5A reconnaissance Lightning was despatched at 0747 from Guadalcanal to the Kahili area to report on the weather and then the results of the strike. This was conducted by Lieutenant Ardall Nord who never returned, however the answer to his demise lies in Japanese records. In order to minimise their chances of being surprised, that morning over southern Bougainville Zero unit No. 252 *Ku* had conducted a series of four-aircraft patrols commencing at 0705. The second patrol launched from Ballale at 0911 led by Warrant Officer Hayama Yuritake whose quartet intercepted and claimed a single "P-38" near Bougainville at 0931. When Nord failed to make his scheduled radio call to the unit's HQ at Fighter #2, they knew something was wrong. Hayama's quartet returned to Ballale at 1020, claiming a definite P-38 kill and each having spent about two-thirds of their ammunition in doing so.

Meanwhile the weather was fine with scattered high cloud as Corsairs from VMF-124 led by Major Gise joined ten 339th FS Lightnings to escort nine olive drab VPB-101 PB4Y-1 Liberators which would bomb Japanese shipping anchored off Buin and in the Shortlands. A hornet's nest of Zeros and Rufe floatplanes was about to contest the raid and hound the Americans both over the target and then as they withdrew.

Each Liberator toted a single 1,000-pound General Purpose bomb. The bombers were led from squadron code 51-P-1 flown by the unit commander, Lieutenant-Commander William Moffett Jr. The Liberators still retained the "51" designator prefix from when the unit had previously been VP-51. P-38G and -F Lightnings flew high cover, and launched mid-morning led by Captain James Geyer, accompanied by a dozen F4Us of VMF-124. The Lightnings would fly

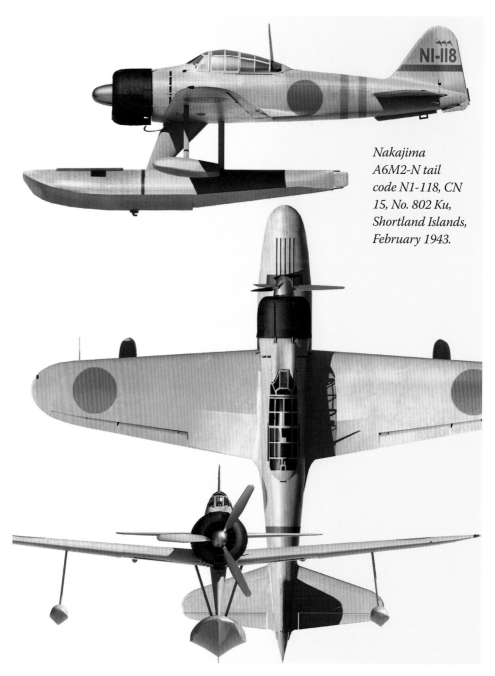

Nakajima A6M2-N tail code N1-118, CN 15, No. 802 Ku, Shortland Islands, February 1943.

This Rufe was one of four survivors of the Yokohama Ku most of whose inventory was destroyed at Tulagi by American strafing in August 1942. After regrouping and reorganisation, on 26 August these four survivors were moved to the Shortlands. On 1 September they were reassigned to the Kamikawa Maru flight detachment led by Lieutenant Horihashi Takeshi where CN 15 received two yellow fuselage bands to designate the unit. On 1 November 1942 all floatplanes based in Rabaul and in the Solomons were brought under the umbrella of the newly formed No. 802 Ku. Accordingly, the fuselage bands were painted over with olive-gray paint and the new tail code applied, the prefix N1 representing No. 802 Ku, part of Rear Admiral Jojima Takatsugu's R-Area Force.

Lieutenant Miyano Zenjiro when he was a cadet at Eta Jima Naval Academy. The two kanji characters represent the surname Miyano.

high cover while the Corsairs would fly alongside the bombers. Both fighter units were based at Fighter #2 (Kukum Field) on Guadalcanal.

Meanwhile the third No. 252 *Ku* Zero patrol had been airborne over southern Bougainville for about forty minutes led by FPO2c Okabayashi Tamotsu when it spotted the incoming Americans. Okabayashi broadcast a warning call resulting in an intense scramble from Ballale airfield. Leading Airman Matsuda Genichi hit a tree on take-off due to impaired visibility caused by raised dust. The impact flipped his Zero however a shaken Matsuda was unhurt, protected by the roll-bar feature incorporated into all A6M series airframes except the Rufe. His Zero however was a write-off.

Ten minutes before opening bomb doors, from high above the American pilots watched dust rise from Kahili airfield as more Zeros scrambled. These were thirteen No. 204 *Ku* fighters led by the unit's *buntaicho*, the redoubtable Lieutenant Miyano Zenjiro. During the bomb run, while the Zeros were still climbing to engage, the Liberators were bracketed by anti-aircraft fire from ships at anchor and shore batteries. Below the Buin-Shortland anchorage offered a rich suite of shipping targets including *Hitachi Maru, Kisaragi Maru, Toyu Maru, Nissan Maru No.3, Hibari Maru, Nojima Maru* and a hodgepodge of subchasers. Bombs were released at 1145 but despite generous claims only one ship was lost. This was the 6,500-ton merchantman *Hitachi Maru* anchored off Kahili when two near-misses split the hull and killed four sailors. The damaged vessel was beached by her captain near Moila Point on south Bougainville's shore where the cargo was salvaged. *Kisaragi Maru*, nearby at anchor, was slightly damaged by near misses.

The first aerial combat occurred when the Lightnings dived towards the climbing No. 204 *Ku* Zeros. While Miyano's flyers were hell-bent on reaching the Liberators, another unconventional fighter unit was scrambling from Shortlands harbour. This comprised eleven No. 802 *Ku*

The first publicly released photo of Corsairs in the Pacific shows those of VMF-124 lined up at Kukum Field on Guadalcanal in February 1943.

Zero pilots wait for a mission briefing on Bougainville in 1943.

A6M2-N Rufes led by their *buntaicho* Lieutenant (jg) Yokoyama Takeshi. Among Yokoyama's pilots was another officer, Lieutenant (jg) Yamazaki Keizo, however the airborne cadre was reduced to ten when FPO1c Hirana Mikazu returned to base with a faulty engine. The others joined the fray with the thirteen airborne No. 204 *Ku* Zeros and eighteen more from No. 252 *Ku* based at Ballale airfield. This totaled 41 Japanese fighters ready to contest Bougainville airspace.

After the bomb run the Liberators banked left for the return journey however both Zeros and floatplanes relentlessly pressed attacks against the Americans. A furious dogfight developed as the bomber formation withdrew to the southeast. The first casualty was a PB4Y hit squarely in the cockpit from a head-on pass which drove it into the sea south of the Shortlands. This attack was made by both Miyano's No. 204 *Ku* flyers and Yokoyama's Rufes, marking the end of Liberator 51-P-3 flown by Stuart Cooper, a pilot who enjoyed hero status within the squadron. When previously flying with VP-51, it had been Cooper's crew who found and helped rescue a ditched Liberator crew from the middle of the Pacific Ocean on 6 June 1942. Meanwhile more Japanese tore into another Liberator, hitting it badly. This was 51-P-4 flown by Lieutenant Jay Bacon Jr which struggled towards home, but never made it. Instead Bacon was forced to ditch the cripple some twelve miles off New Georgia.

Three Lightning pilots were lost in the resultant fierce and widespread melee: Lieutenants Joseph Finkenstein, Wellman Huey and Donald White. No-one could pin-point who was lost where or even how, and another Lightning pilot Lieutenant John Mulvey ditched due to combat damage when his power finally gave out close to home base. He was rescued near Russell Island the next day, but not so pilots of the two VMF-124 Corsairs lost, Bu. No. 02187 flown by Lieutenant Gordon Lyon, Jr and Bu. No. 02249 flown by Lieutenant Harold Stewart.

Stewart was particularly unfortunate. He re-joined element leader Lieutenant Lloyd Pearson after a combat engagement at about 20,000 feet. When he pulled up alongside, Pearson could

A P-38G assigned to the 339th Fighter Squadron at Kukum Field in early April 1943.

see vapour trails of gasoline spraying from several jagged bullet holes which laced Stewart's wing, although Stewart himself appeared okay. The streaming fuel saw the Corsair run dry about ten minutes later whereupon Stewart waved farewell and gently nosed down to ditch. He was followed by enemy fighters, quick to sense a cripple. Although Stewart ditched cleanly, and Pearson saw a yellow life raft appear beside the aircraft, the following Zeros strafed the raft. Stewart was never seen again.

Yokoyama's No. 802 *Ku* Rufes commenced combat from 1210, some fighting for more than half an hour, during which the bomber chase and numerous dogfights scattered them badly. The first returned to Shortland harbour at 1315 and the last 25 minutes later. Incredibly, not one Rufe had been hit, a reflection of pilot skill and the nimbleness of the well-designed floatplane, doubtless with a touchstone of luck as well. It is difficult to ascertain which Japanese pilots were responsible for what: No. 252 *Ku* claimed one B-24, eight P-38s, one P-39 and two F4Us as definite, while No. 204 *Ku* claimed one B-24, one P-38, two P-39s and one F4U.

The Marine Corsairs claimed three Zeros and a "Pete", the PB4Y gunners nine Zeros, and Lightning pilot Captain Bill Griffith one fighter. However, against fourteen American claims the only Japanese loss was No. 252 *Ku* pilot FPO2c Yoshida Yoshio who collided with Lyon's Corsair during the dogfight. Two No. 252 *Ku* Zeros suffered gunfire hits, injuring both pilots but both landed safely. The unit's eighteen Zeros had fired the considerable sum of 5,126 x 7.7 mm and 1,369 x 20mm rounds of ammunition, reflecting intense combat.

Thus, the first Corsair combat proved a fiasco with the Americans losing nine aircraft: one F5A, four P-38s, two Corsairs and two Liberators. The debacle, which became known throughout the theatre as the "Saint Valentine's Day Massacre", showcased Japanese fighter tactics. It also underlined the potency of the Rufe, a key player in the engagement. American losses were of sufficient magnitude that further daylight missions against the Bougainville area were discontinued until fighter tactics could be reassessed. Night bombing attacks resumed against Bougainville, but for the next month both Corsair and P-38 combat engagements in the Solomons theatre were restrained while the Americans mulled over their future operational doctrine.

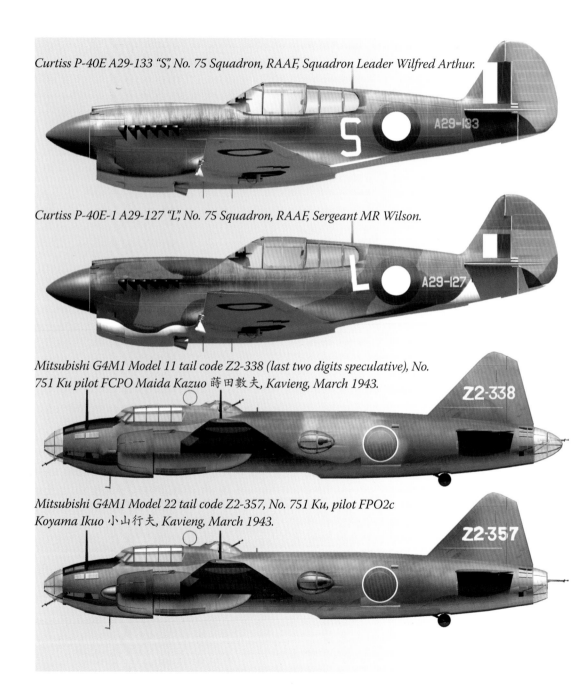

Curtiss P-40E A29-133 "S", No. 75 Squadron, RAAF, Squadron Leader Wilfred Arthur.

Curtiss P-40E-1 A29-127 "L", No. 75 Squadron, RAAF, Sergeant MR Wilson.

Mitsubishi G4M1 Model 11 tail code Z2-338 (last two digits speculative), No. 751 Ku pilot FCPO Maida Kazuo 蒔田數夫, Kavieng, March 1943.

Mitsubishi G4M1 Model 22 tail code Z2-357, No. 751 Ku, pilot FPO2c Koyama Ikuo 小山行夫, Kavieng, March 1943.

CHAPTER 7
Disappearing Betty

The fate of a lone Betty which never returned from a reconnaissance mission in March 1943 has been resolved after matching Allied and Japanese records.

On 10 March 1943, a No. 751 *Ku* Betty on a long-range sector patrol failed to return. It was one of a pair of Bettys which took off from Kavieng five minutes apart commencing 0600 that morning, each with a crew of eight. FPO2c Koyama Ikuo piloted the first aircraft and scoured area F2 reporting nothing. The Betty which disappeared was piloted and commanded by FCPO Maida Kazuo. It departed five minutes after Koyama and headed for Sector F1. Both these large sectors reached out towards Milne Bay. This chapter aligns hunters and victims for the first time.

The Allied protectors of Milne Bay in March 1943 were the Kittyhawks of Nos. 75 and 77 Squadrons, RAAF. No. 75 Squadron was operating P-40Es and had just returned to New Guinea after a few months in Australia. No. 77 Squadron had recently been transferred to Milne Bay from the Darwin area, and was equipped with a fresh inventory of new P-40Ks, essentially an upgraded "E" model with a more powerful engine and modified fin. On this morning the CO of No. 75 Squadron, Squadron Leader Wilfred Arthur, was conducting a patrol with Sergeant MR Wilson as wingman.

The pair were flying at 21,000 feet north of Fergusson Island when they sighted Maida's Betty flying on an easterly heading at an estimated 17,000 feet. Both Kittyhawks dropped belly tanks and dived left towards the Betty which Wilson reported as having green/brown camouflage. We take up reports from the two RAAF pilots which provide a detailed viewpoint of the close-fought attack.

Firstly, from Squadron Leader Arthur:

> I sighted an aircraft about 7 or 8 miles away against a bank of cumulus cloud flying towards us at about 17,000 feet. We were well above and up sun from the aircraft, so I kept in position as I knew that a friendly aircraft was carrying out a photographic reconnaissance in the area. When I could see that it was a twin engined aircraft I called up No. 2 and we took up position - dropping belly tanks – and on definitely identifying it as a Betty attacked from the port beam - steep climbing attack. I got in a good burst and immediately afterwards the tail gunner *[author's comment: this was FPO1c Takai Atsumu]* stopped firing and did not start again (twin guns with short barrels). At the beginning what looked like a large number of small bombs were dropped as the big bomb doors remained open . . . My guns stopped and I reloaded and attacked again several times from the same position but could only get one gun going.

Kittyhawk pilots relax at Milne Bay just before a scramble in March 1943.

Enemy aircraft was heading northeast and diving slightly towards bank of cloud. Recharged guns and started after aircraft – got within range - (overtaking fairly rapidly) as he entered cloud fired a short burst and then pulled away to the starboard as he disappeared. As he emerged from the other side I was in a good position for a starboard bow attack which I commenced from about 400 yards and closed in as much as possible breaking off at about 70 yards. Saw tracer entering starboard engine and fuselage about one third away from nose. Guns again stopped but I got three going again and made final attack from quarter closing in to about 15 yards in stern position. Gunner about midway up aircraft was firing wildly *[author's comment: – this position was manned by Superior Airman Udo Miyaichi who doubled as the radio operator]* - rear guns still pointing towards the sky. Saw tracer entering fuselage. Pulled away to starboard and saw him turn and go into the sea. Flew low over wreckage which burnt for a few seconds only. Two black objects which looked like the main wheels left floating in the oil and some yellow substance in the water. Big cloud of smoke left over the wreckage which remained there until we were south of Normanby Island on the way home.

Sergeant Wilson reported:

The red markings against the green-brown camouflage stood out very plainly. After the CO attacked the enemy aircraft I made a slow turn from an east to a northeast direction. I made a rear quarter attack but observed tracers going just underneath the enemy aircraft. There was some fire from tail and blister but appeared inaccurate. Enemy aircraft was approaching a bank of cumulus cloud but made no attempt to enter it. At a gap in a cloud after the CO made a couple more attacks I made a beam attack from 300 yards but observed no hits. The enemy aircraft was now in a shallow dive with its tail gun silenced. After the CO made another attack I came in on its stern and followed it from 500 yards to 150 yards. There was no answering fire at this stage. I noticed a few small pieces fly off the enemy aircraft as a result of my fire. Then the starboard motor caught fire. I broke away to the port and noticed that the altimeter read 2,000 feet. The enemy aircraft was now burning underneath the flames starting about the trailing edge of the wing and extending to the tail. Still in a shallow dive the enemy aircraft struck the water and appeared to explode. The flames remained on the water for less than a minute and on a closer examination I could see a few pieces of wreckage floating in yellowish-green pitch.

Notes on No. 751 *Ku* markings

Wilson's contact report describes his quarry as having brown and green camouflage. A limited number of Model 11 Bettys painted in the China scheme survived into 1943 at Rabaul. If Wilson was right (and he got in very close to the Betty), this likely indicates an early Model 11 transferred into the No. 751 *Ku* inventory after No. 4 *Ku* departed the theatre in November 1942. Although No. 751 *Ku*'s unit log for 10 March fails to list the two tail codes for the mission, FPO2c Koyama Ikuo had flown tail code #357 during the five days previous. Crews usually stayed with the same aircraft, availability permitting, so it is likely he was flying the same bomber on the patrol as portrayed here. Two units, No. 253 *Ku* (tail prefix Z1) and No. 751 *Ku* (tail prefix Z2) comprised the 21st *Koku Sentai* which fell under the command of the South East Area Fleet. The Z2 prefix was dropped around late April 1943 so that the unit's bombers appeared with just a three-digit number. The prefix "51" was applied to No. 751 *Ku* bombers towards the end of 1943.

Kittyhawk A29-143 "G" named PUDDIN, of No. 75 Squadron, RAAF, at Milne Bay.

Douglas P-70 serial 39-768 Dusty, 6th NFS Detachment A, Kila 'drome, Port Moresby, March 1943.

Douglas P-70 serial 39-774, 6th NFS, Detachment B, Guadalcanal, April 1943.

A P-70 on finals at Kila 'drome, Port Moresby.

CHAPTER 8
Nighthawk Night Fighters

Radar-equipped Douglas P-70 Nighthawks were deployed to both Guadalcanal and Port Moresby as night fighters in 1943. They were ill-suited as fighters, having a slow rate of climb and a limited ceiling, but surprisingly managed at least two successes.

The USAAF had no night fighter units when the US entered the war, however in 1942 a night fighter training organisation was established at Orlando, Florida. There, Douglas P-70s (modified A-20A Havocs) were used to develop tactics for radar-controlled night interceptions, and ultimately to train crews to populate nineteen USAAF night fighter squadrons. The first P-70 was delivered to the USAAF in April 1942, and was allocated the official name "Nighthawk", however the name never really caught on.

The first units to deploy the P-70 to the Pacific were Detachments A and B of the 6th Night Fighter Squadron. Detachment B went to Guadalcanal with the Thirteenth Air Force, while A served with the Fifth Air Force in New Guinea for eight months but was later recalled to Hawaii. The first P-70 mission on Guadalcanal was flown on 1 April 1943, in conjunction with an example of the latest technology radar, callsign Kiwi, operated by New Zealand personnel. This new technology had just arrived in April 1943 and was termed Ground Control Interception (GCI) radar, customised to work with P-70 night fighters.

Detachment A departed Hawaii on 18 February 1943, with six P-70As and two Liberator LB30 mother ships to carry supplies and navigate. One P-70A was lost en route, due to a mid-air collision in poor visibility. The remaining five diverted via Espirito Santo where their long-range bomb-bay fuel tanks were replaced by electronic equipment. The five proceeded to Port Moresby's Three-Mile 'drome (Kila) a few days later, staging via Milne Bay. At Kila, they operated under Fifth Fighter Command, where they shared the dirt strip mainly with fighter units.

None of the 6th NFS pilots was enthusiastic about flying the P-70, largely as all had previously trained on fighters in the US. They openly discussed how they would rather be flying the Lightnings parked on the other side of the field. They quickly discovered that their P-70As had trouble gaining sufficient altitude to intercept enemy bombers, always Rabaul-based G4M1 Bettys, thus limiting opportunities for a kill. The P-70's poor climb performance was the major reason why it floundered as a night fighter in the view of pilot First Lieutenant John Florence:

> Operationally, with only five P-70s, our mission was to intercept bombers sent over our area at night. Since we could not get up to where they were, regular patrols were out of the question. When our ground radar picked up an inbound enemy flight over the Owen Stanley Mountains, we would scramble only one aircraft, and on most occasions it was futile. Our standard operating procedure was to fly a couple of P-70s over to nearby Seven Mile 'drome every evening, and then return after sunrise. The strategy behind this was strictly for our

A No. 702 Ku Betty has its engine changed at Vunakanau.

own safety, as we needed the longer runway, and Three Mile Strip had hills in the area.

As night attackers, Japanese bomber crews had their own challenges. Whilst they tried to plan night missions on bright moonlight nights to enhance visibility, tropical weather often conspired against them. As a result, of 45 sorties launched against Port Moresby between 10 to 24 May 1943, fifteen were aborted outright after departing Rabaul, and sixteen failed to cross the Owen Stanley mountains due to weather. In such cases the Japanese instead bombed alternative targets on New Guinea's north coast, however this was really just an excuse to dump bombs. For some reason No. 702 *Ku hikotaicho* Captain Sumida Shinhichi decided that the night missions would benefit from the expertise of his senior officers, and this was showcased on the evening of 15 May 1943 as we shall see.

From the beginning of their Pacific deployments, doubt lingered about how the P-70's radar would perform in the heat and humidity of tropical climate, doubt which manifested itself early. Accurately interpreting target azimuth and elevation required patient radar operators. Since P-70 pilots had no radar scope in front of them, the operators acted as their "eyes". Interception

Douglas P-70 Dusty from Detachment A has an engine change at Kila 'drome in March 1943. This aircraft was destroyed in an accident at Townsville shortly afterwards.

The radio operator position in the G4M1. This crew member also fired the dorsal guns.

thus relied heavily on crew coordination, and given the poor performance of the fledgling radar, this collaboration was often sorely tested. Nonetheless the Pacific P-70s scored two successful kills.

Its first success in the Pacific theatre occurred over Guadalcanal in the early hours of 19 April 1943, credited to Captain Earl Bennett. The Betty crews of No. 705 *Ku* had taken a beating in previous weeks due to their involvement in the two biggest I-Go *Sakusen* missions, Port Moresby and Milne Bay. Whilst its sister unit No. 751 *Ku* stood down afterwards for nearly two weeks while its bombers were patched up at Kavieng and its aircrews took leave in Tinian, No. 705 *Ku* did not enjoy the same level of reprieve. It continued operations with sector patrols then recommenced combat with an unusual mission format against Guadalcanal on 18 April, sending five pairs of Bettys over the island at night from 2215 until 0210 dropping mixes of 60- and 250-kilogram bombs. On this night it lost observer Warrant Officer Furuya Sadao and crew over Guadalcanal, after it was intercepted by Bennett at 22,000 feet. This occurred after Bennett's struggling P-70 took 45 minutes to reach that altitude. Furuya's bomber was held captive in searchlights for five minutes before Bennett attacked.

In subsequent interceptions at ceiling altitude in similar circumstances over Guadalcanal, it was clear the Japanese learned from experience. When a P-70 closed in, the Japanese simply outran the attacker by entering a shallow dive. As a result, the P-70s changed their tactics and patrolled an outer zone under radar coverage while P-38s set up an inner attack zone aided by searchlights.

The first P-70 success in New Guinea took place a month later, on 15 May 1943, and was credited to Lieutenant Burrell Adams with Flying Officer Paul DiLabbio as radar operator. On this particular evening, Port Moresby received ample warning of an imminent night attack. Bulldog and Rouna outposts reported that bogeys were headed south at 1910. Radar tracking commenced eight minutes later, and soon a Japanese formation of six G4M1s overflew Moresby from the southwest.

The six No. 702 *Ku* bombers were under the overall command of *hikotaicho* Captain Sumida Shinhichi whose crew of eight had departed Vunakanau at 1555. Their mission was to bomb Port Moresby's airfields with 60-kilogram bombs while flying in three pairs. Sumida's partner that evening was another Betty flown by FPO1c Yamakizaki Mamoru.

Times for the contact quoted in Japanese records coincide precisely with USAAF records. Adams closed in on Sumida's duo from 12,000 feet after they had dropped their bombs over Durand 'drome. Sumida made several runs over the target, in an apparent effort to ensure bombing accuracy. In doing so, he became more vulnerable to the P-70's guns and was aware he was being stalked and fired upon. Indeed, his radio-operator Warrant Officer Akiyoshi Kiyohito managed to radio Rabaul at 1949 that the pair was under attack. Sumida's Betty quickly fell.

His partner Yamakizaki's gunners returned fire at the P-70, expending 127 x 20mm and 620 x 7.7mm rounds, however none hit the American. After several passes at the Bettys, Adams reported that he had shot down a "Sally" bomber 35 miles northwest of Seven-Mile 'drome at 2005. After Adams returned home, two more pairs of No. 702 *Ku* Bettys soon appeared over Port Moresby at 2030 and 2050. Remarkably both were flown by senior flag officers, Commanders Yatsukida Kyoshi and Takahama Haruo. The five remaining Bettys returned home safely and landed between 2300 and 0015.

Despite these kills the limitations of the P-70 as a night interceptor were readily apparent. As a result, Detachment A was transferred back to Hawaii from Port Moresby, and Detachment B conducted harassment missions from Guadalcanal instead of night interdictions. These ranged as far as Bougainville and even Rabaul. In their final days in theatre some P-70s even took part in daylight strafing missions.

The first P-70s to arrive in New Guinea are seen refueling at Seven-Mile in late February 1943.

A No. 702 Ku Betty tail code 326 in a Vunakanau revetment in 1943.

F4U-1 #18 Bubbles, VMF-124, Guadalcanal, June 1943.

F4F-4 F-21, VF-11, Lieutenant (jg) William Leonard, Guadalcanal, June 1943.

P-39D serial #41-38400, squadron #56, 68th FS, 347th FG, Guadalcanal, June 1943.

A6M3 Model 22 unknown tail code, No. 204 Ku, unidentified chutaicho, June 1943.

A6M3 Model 22 tail code 173, No. 582 Ku, hikotaicho Lieutenant Shindo Saburo 進藤三朗, June 1943.

CHAPTER 9
Ace in a Day?

In June 1943 a large Japanese formation, comprising 92 aircraft, attacked targets near Guadalcanal. It was contested by over 100 Allied fighters who took a heavy toll on the Japanese crews. Pilot Murray Shubin was awarded five kills and famously became an "Ace in a Day", but what evidence supports his claim?

When Lightning pilot Lieutenant Murray Shubin was awarded five Zero kills on 16 June 1943 over Guadalcanal he became the Thirteenth's Air Force's first "Ace in a Day". On this day the Japanese made their second biggest air-raid against Guadalcanal after the Operation I-Go mission of 7 April 1943. Two dozen D3A2 Val dive-bombers with substantial fighter escort came to Guadalcanal to attack USN shipping. During 45 minutes of close combat, American and RNZAF fighters exacted a heavy toll, although nowhere near the numbers claimed.

As always with Guadalcanal air battles at this middle stage of the Pacific war, air combat was supplemented by heavy and often accurate AA fire, both land-based and from ships. Total US claims bordered on the fanciful: 79 Japanese aircraft to air combat and 28 to AA fire (all types). This was a total of 107 enemy aircraft, more than were airborne! In fact "only" ten Vals and fourteen Zeros were shot down during aerial combat, with three more Vals brought down by ship-borne AA for a total loss of 27 aircraft. The Allied fighters thus over-claimed by more than six to one (Japanese claims were even more exaggerated). Although six US fighters were lost, only two fell to combat with one of those pilots rescued. Disturbingly, the other four were due to mid-air collisions.

First indication of the incoming raid was provided by coastwatchers at Vella Lavella, confirmed by Guadalcanal's radar not long after. The sizeable Japanese force appeared on radar scopes to be originally divided between a combined force of two dozen No. 582 *Ku* D3A2 Val dive-bombers with sixteen escorting Zeros from the same unit, bolstered by separate formations of two dozen No. 204 *Ku* and thirty No. 251 *Ku* Zeros, a total of 92 aircraft. The composite fighter contingent fell under the command of Lieutenant-Commander Shindo Saburo, *hikotaicho* of No. 582 *Ku*. The two lagging Zero formations flew slightly above and behind the dive-bombers, closing up as they approached Guadalcanal.

Captain Kodo Kei led the Val contingent, however the Vals were particularly sluggish as each was weighed down heavily with one 250-kilogram bomb under the fuselage and two 60-kilogram bombs under each wing pylon. Such a maximum bomb load configuration was not often used.

The No. 251 *Ku* Zeros were led by Lieutenant O'ono Takeyoshi (previously of Tainan *Ku* fame), most of which had arrived at Buin from Rabaul where they refuelled and set off again just after midday. An advance No. 251 *Ku* detachment based at Buka had shot down a Fortress earlier that morning, and had flown to Buin to join the current formation. The two dozen No. 204

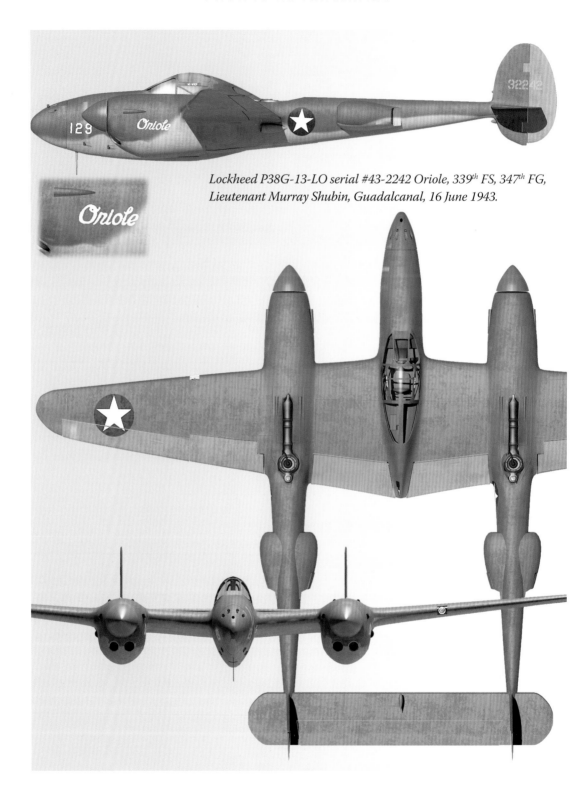

Lockheed P38G-13-LO serial #43-2242 Oriole, 339th FS, 347th FG,
Lieutenant Murray Shubin, Guadalcanal, 16 June 1943.

Ku Zeros led by *hikotaicho* Lieutenant Miyano Zenjiro had also flown to Buin from Rabaul very early that morning where, alongside their No. 251 *Ku* comrades, they had refuelled and departed for the mission.

As they had done before, the Japanese approached Guadalcanal by skirting the Russell Islands, then cruised between Savo Island and Cape Esperance at around 25,000 feet, the effective service ceiling for the fully loaded Vals. Since there was little USN shipping in the harbour, at least compared to recent months, the Americans first thought that the intended target was airfields and ground installations. Fighter Direction vectored a total of 104 American and RNZAF fighters to several locations to deal with any eventuality. Thus the Russells, Cape Esperance, Tulagi and Henderson Field were each stacked with waiting and staggered fighter formations. Additional fighter reserves were placed to guard shipping anchorages. This was always going to be a big fight.

Ten 339th FS P-38s led by Lieutenant William Griffith were first to make contact with the incoming enemy formation. A fight unfolded over Beaufort Bay area at 25,000 feet, drawing many of the Zeros to the north as the dive-bombers continued unimpeded over the mountains. The No. 251 *Ku* Zeros threw themselves into the scrap along with those No. 204 *Ku* Zeros not engaged in guarding the Vals. O'ono claimed five Lightings no less! After breaking free from the Lightnings many No. 251 *Ku* Zeros followed the Vals over towards Lunga where, along with the No. 204 *Ku* Zeros, they now engaged Wildcats, P-39s and P-40s.

The Wildcats were initially a dozen from VF-11 led by Lieutenant-Commander Charles White whose charges had been vectored across the mountains from Henderson Field. The Wildcats were at 25,000 feet when they first saw the combined No. 582 *Ku* enemy force estimated at fifty planes, and fell into combat shortly after the Lightnings. In the ensuing actions they claimed thirteen dive-bombers and eight Zeros with no losses. VF-11 pilots Lieutenants Charles Stimpson and Jim Swope were awarded four and three dive-bombers respectively. Swope's Wildcat was torn up by about 40 bullets and two 20mm hits to his engine which blew off three cylinders. He limped back about twenty miles to Fighter #1 where his Grumman was junked.

In this first action the 339th FS Lightnings claimed eleven Zeros for no losses. The engagement was highlighted by Lieutenant Murray "Jim" Shubin, who claimed five of these during forty minutes of combat. Flying P-38G #129 *Oriole*, Shubin made full use of the heavy Lightning's superior speed with multiple high speed passes before climbing back to repeat the process each time. Shubin was afterwards proclaimed the Thirteenth's Air Force's first "Ace in a Day".

Sixteen additional Wildcats originally vectored to Beaufort Bay were later redirected to Cape Esperance where they caught four dive-bombers and claimed six Zeros. Some 40 aircraft which formed a collective of eight 68th and 70th FS USAAF P-39D Airacobras and 21 44th FS Warhawks along with eight RNZAF No. 14 Squadron Kittyhawks fought Vals and protective Zeros as shipping was being attacked, and then subsequently when the Japanese retired towards Savo Island.

In addition, flights of Corsairs from VMF-121, VMF-122 and VMF-124 scrambled from

Taken at Buin on 2 June 1943, about a fortnight before the Guadalcanal raid, this photograph shows No. 582 Ku key leaders and pilots. Circled left to right are: Lieutenant Suzuki Usaburo, Commanding Officer Commander Yamamoto Sakae, Hikotaicho Shindo Saburo (sunglasses), Lieutenant Noguchi Gi'ichi, Warrant Officer Tsunoda Kazuo and Warrant Officer Takenaka Yoshihito. Shindo led the fighter contingent on the 16 June 1943 mission.

different bases throughout the engagement. Among five claims by Corsairs, Captain Howard Finn of VMF-124 claimed one dive-bomber and one Zero.

It was No. 582 *Ku* which suffered the first Zero losses, losing four: FPO1c Fukumori Daizo, FPO2c Shinozuba Kenishi, FPO2c Ishibashi Mototami and FPO1c Furumoto Katsumi. Total Zero losses for No. 251 *Ku* were six including two *chutaicho*, Lieutenants O'oya Shuhei and Hoashi Takashi, along with Warrant Officer O'oki Yoshio, FPO2c Yamamoto Suehiro, FPO2c Kanda Hiroshi and FPO2c Shimizu Ikuzo.

After the main fight, *hikotaicho* O'ono led his men directly back to Rabaul where they landed in the dark at 1930, and FPO2c Terada Yukikazo made a wheels-up landing. Another No. 251 *Ku* Zero was scrapped after incurring serious combat damage. Four Zeros fell from No. 204 *Ku*, including Lieutenants Morizaki Takeshi and unit *hikotaicho* Miyano Zenjiro, a legend among the unit's men who had led them in many fights and had enjoyed an exemplary combat career. The other two No. 204 *Ku* pilots lost were FPO2c Tamura Yamato and FPO2c Kanda Saji. Seventeen surviving No. 204 *Ku* Zeros overnighted at Buka, returning to Rabaul next morning. Four more made emergency landings at Buin where one pilot had to be helped from the cockpit due to injuries.

To better understand Shubin's claims we return to when the red alert was sounded at 1346 as

Shubin with his Lightning Oriole at Guadalcanal, just before application of the fifth rising sun victory symbol.

An Airacobra undergoes service on Guadalcanal in mid-1943.

the Vals headed over the mountains from Cape Esperance towards the shipping. While the ships sought sea room in a mild easterly breeze and calm sea, their sailors sighted the first dive-bombers at 1410 when a dozen appeared in a vee formation through a gap in the cloud 15,000 feet above. The Vals dived in train, then pulled out at about 500 feet after which they commenced strafing attacks. The second *chutai* of a dozen Vals was also led by a senior *chutaicho* flag officer with rank of captain (name undecipherable). They followed shortly thereafter, during which this *chutaicho* was one of those lost.

The Vals hit cargo ship USS *Celeno* (AK-76) aft, resulting in black billowing smoke, however the damage was soon contained. Another Val crashed into an LST which was already beached and unloading. Combined bombing and strafing attacks resulted in 25 US sailors killed, 29 wounded and 22 missing. This was the total damage inflicted by an attack whose main purpose was to sink shipping. At 1420 other Vals were reported over Tulagi, but no damage to shipping ensued. Of the many claims submitted against the Vals by ships' gunnery, three were confirmed as witnessed by many. Credit goes to destroyer USS *Strong* (DD-467) which in seven minutes of focused ship-borne gunnery fired 194 x 5-inch, 750 x 40mm and 980 x 20mm rounds. When each Val was hit it streamed thick black smoke. The first lost control and fell into the water, the second exploded from a direct hit, and the third crashed in flames, before pluming thick black smoke from the water.

The widespread and intense nature of the attack produced several noteworthy and curious incidents:

- When Lieutenant Bill Harris let down into the circuit area in P-38 *Hattie* he was strafed by a Zero. Harris was so incensed he grabbed another Lightning ready on standby, however he aborted the take-off when he blew a main tyre.

- RNZAF P-40K Kittyhawk NZ3056 had an engine failure during the scramble and landed on a nearby beach undamaged. It was shortly thereafter returned to service

- Only two flights of VMF-122 Corsairs were scrambled. Lieutenant EE Shifflett claimed a Zero from the same encounter where Technical Sergeant Thomas Efstathiou was bounced by another and cleanly shot into the ocean.

- Four US fatalities resulted from mid-air collisions. P-40 pilot Lieutenant John Tedder collided with VF-11 Wildcat pilot Teddy Hull when intercepting the same Zero. Then, VF-11 Wildcat pilots Lieutenants Chandler Boswell and George Ricker collided with each other pursuing another Zero low over the water.

- VF-11 Wildcat pilot Lieutenant John Pressler was forced to ditch suddenly when his engine seized. He was soon rescued.

- Two sections of VMF-121 Corsairs scrambled from the Russells at 1300, made no contact and returned at 1500. A solitary VMF-121 Corsair flown by Lieutenant William Rhodes scrambled at 1400, and climbed to 9,000 to join with other Corsairs but could not locate them. Just as he decided to return to base he nearly collided with the falling wreckage of a flaming Zero.

- Admiral "Bull" Halsey was so impressed with Shubin's alleged five kills that he subsequently invited him to his flagship to present him the Distinguished Service Cross.

Did Shubin really shoot down five Zeros? His own combat report cites two definites and four probables, yet he saw none of the probables crash. Furthermore, his descriptions of these incidents reflect standard Japanese combat tactics at this stage of the war:

> . . . first turned on its back, hung for a moment, and did the first half of a split S (first claim) . . . slipped into a vertical turn and peeled off going down, apparently under control except for his engine (second claim) . . . he was smoking and still on his back when I passed over him. I never saw him again (third claim) . . . he was diving straight as I passed over. I pulled out levelled up and turned to catch sight, but I could see nothing (fourth claim) . . .

Three confirmed kills were allegedly witnessed through binoculars by a 35th Infantry Regiment officer on Guadalcanal, Captain FP Mueller, however Mueller fails to explain how he identified Shubin's Lightning (named *Oriole* on the cowl), when Shubin's engagements commenced about ten miles out at sea heading for Savo Island. In the event, Mueller's report to Shubin's CO, Colonel Aaron Tyler, convinced Thirteenth Fighter Command to award Shubin five confirmed kills against claims of two definites. Many other Allied pilots submitted numerous and more detailed claims than Shubin against Zeros, especially the VF-11 Wildcats which appear to have been the most successful type engaged in combat that day.

The facts are that the 339th Lightning pilots were awarded eleven Zeros between them, including five to Shubin. Total Allied awards for the day were, inter alia, 49 Zero kills to all Allied fighters, compared to actual losses of fourteen. The odds against one pilot scoring five of these are most improbable. Put another way, if it is the case that one Allied fighter of the 104 airborne scored five kills it means that Shubin alone would have scored more than one third of all the Zeros shot down that day. Against the consideration of the other confirmed kills, it seems more likely that Shubin scored one or perhaps two kills, and the other Lightnings scored a further two perhaps three, with some of these being the ones witnessed by Mueller.

USS Celeno (AK-76) off Guadalcanal shortly before it was hit by Vals.

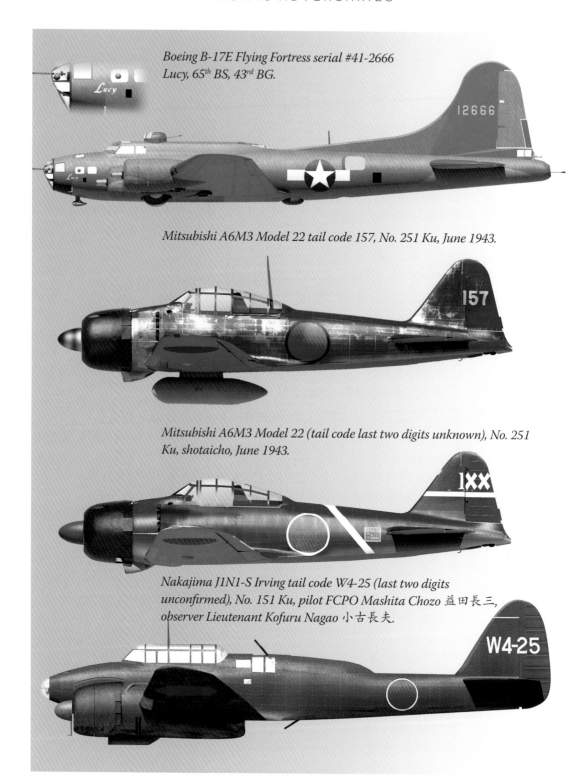

Boeing B-17E Flying Fortress serial #41-2666
Lucy, 65th BS, 43rd BG.

Mitsubishi A6M3 Model 22 tail code 157, No. 251 Ku, June 1943.

Mitsubishi A6M3 Model 22 (tail code last two digits unknown), No. 251
Ku, shotaicho, June 1943.

Nakajima J1N1-S Irving tail code W4-25 (last two digits
unconfirmed), No. 151 Ku, pilot FCPO Mashita Chozo 益田長三,
observer Lieutenant Kofuru Nagao 小古長夫.

CHAPTER 10
Dual Medal of Honor Fortress

A combat-worn B-17E Flying Fortress is tasked with dangerous solo photo reconnaissance sorties over enemy bases. After running into Zeros over Buka, the plane is badly shot up and the wounded crew just manage to nurse their crippled bomber back to Dobodura. The aircrew became the most decorated crew in US military history with awards including two Medals of Honor.

Zero pilot Warrant Officer O'oki Yoshio flew two fateful combat missions on 16 June 1943. On the first he was instrumental in the creation of two Medal of Honor awardees, one of whom would live another 64 years. The second mission cost O'oki his life that same afternoon. O'oki joined the IJN as a fireman at the age of seventeen, changed to a mechanic, and then graduated as a fighter pilot at age twenty-one. He served in China as one of Japan's first Zero pilots and then joined the famed Tainan *Ku* at Rabaul in July 1942. He flew several Guadalcanal missions with this unit, returned to Japan in November, then returned to Rabaul in May 1943. There he was assigned to No. 251 *Ku* where he regularly flew as a *shotaicho*, but because of his considerable experience he also sometimes flew in a *chutaicho* capacity.

As part of planning for Operation Cartwheel, the scheme to neutralise Rabaul, as early as June 1943 plans were being drawn up for a landing at Torokina on Bougainville later that year. Reconnaissance of the large island fell under the purview of the Fifth Air Force and obtaining photos of the expanded Japanese air base at Buka became a priority. At this stage of the war Buka boasted an extensive system of revetments which protected a coterie of aggressors which had the potential to disrupt the planned invasion. The photographic task was assigned to the 43rd BG which would use a converted Flying Fortress as a more stable and better-equipped photographic platform than the F-5 Lightning.

The Group's Commanding Officer, Major Harry Hawthorne, knew the unescorted mission could be especially dangerous and so called for volunteers. Captain Jay Zeamer, the 65th BS Executive Officer, was the first to volunteer and his crew immediately fell behind him. Zeamer had more experience than anyone else in the group with solo reconnaissance missions: he had flown three in the past month alone. Zeamer was assigned a modified -E model Fortress recently named *Lucy* for the task. It been converted into a photo reconnaissance platform when temporarily assigned to the 8th PRS before being returned to the 43rd BG to perform the same duties. The old bomber had a poor reputation with crews, as it appeared to attract more than its fair share of bad luck. Among several hard luck incidents, in November 1942 its life raft had accidentally deployed, damaging the tailplane and causing an early return to base. Furthermore, some crew viewed the last three digits of its serial number – 666 – as bad luck.

The Fortress had been substantially modified for its solo role. A trimetrogon camera system allowed the creation of mosaics for generating photo maps, and new engines had recently been fitted for optimum performance. The bomber was stripped of all extra weight and fortified

FCPO Mashita Chozo guides his J1N1-C Irving past Zeamer's Fortress for a close-range inspection.

Zero pilot Warrant Officer O'oki Yoshio in early 1943.

with additional dual 0.50-inch calibre Brownings in both the radio compartment and dorsal positions. A final touch was an additional fixed 0.50-inch gun in the nose operated from the pilot's control column.

Lucy launched from Port Moresby's Seven-Mile 'drome an hour before sunrise on Wednesday 16 June 1943 and headed directly for Buka. The distance of just over 500 miles put the target on the limits of its fuel range and required that an extra fuselage fuel tank be fitted. In fine weather at exactly 0800 it was overhead Buka at 25,000 feet for the first of several photo runs. The task would require about twenty minutes of slow and steady passes in multiple directions. Forewarned, below at Buka eight No. 251 *Ku* Model 22 Zeros scrambled to intercept *Lucy* led by Warrant Officer O'oki Yoshio. Standard operating procedure was for a full *chutai* of nine fighters to launch, however one Zero from O'oki's *chutai* was down for maintenance. The contingent was operating from Buka as an advance contingent from Rabaul.

For Zeamer and his crew who saw the Zeros scramble, this was now a race against time. The stable flightpath of Zeamer's Fortress gave O'oki's flyers time to climb and then pull ahead of the Fortress. There they positioned themselves for a head-on attack: O'oki and two wingmen, FPO2c Yamamoto Suehiro and FPO2c Terada Koichi, led the first strike. O'oki selected his cannon for the first pass, during which his wing sustained return fire from one of the Fortress' gunners. After he swept past, O'oki banked and dived steeply left, his mount sufficiently damaged that he elected to return to Buka. He was accompanied by the least-experienced combat pilot, FPO2c Iwano Hiroshi. This was standard operating procedure, for if O'oki were forced to ditch, Iwano would be able to pin-point his position for rescue.

As the remaining six Zeros positioned themselves ahead of *Lucy*, a twin-engine Japanese aircraft made a surprise cameo appearance. It swept past, and the Fortress crew thought it fired at them. Perhaps it did although no ammunition expenditure is recorded which could simply be administrative oversight. In an extraordinary co-incidence, this was a No. 151 *Ku* J1N1-S Irving cruising at high altitude on its own reconnaissance mission. Flown by FCPO Mashita Chozo, it was under the command of Lieutenant Kofuru Nagao who occupied the rear observer's position. Mashita had departed Rabaul that morning at 0520 and was heading for Ballale when he saw the Fortress in the distance. Curiosity took the better of him and he swept past to inspect the four-engine bomber, the first he had ever seen. After the pass he landed at Ballale at 1000 to refuel. He and Kofuru then reconnoitred US shipping around Guadalcanal, returning to Ballale at 1340. After refuelling again, they returned to Rabaul late that afternoon at 1620. It was Mashita's detailed report of shipping numbers anchored off Lunga which precipitated the later Japanese attack in which O'oki was a participant.

After the Irving swept past, the remaining six Zeros conducted a head-on attack, followed by rear and beam attacks against the Fortress. This was a fierce battle which the Japanese records log as of 32 minutes duration from 0843 to 0915. In the process most of the Zero pilots expended their full complement of 160 rounds of 20mm cannon. Despite the Fortress crew claiming five Zeros, the only Japanese loss was FPO2c Yahiro Shinichi, forced to ditch after his engine was hit. Yahiro was rescued and returned to Buka via an IJN launch. A total of three Zeros, including O'oki who returned early to Buka with his shot-up wing, were damaged by gunfire. Finally out of ammunition and running low on fuel, the five remaining Zeros had returned to Buka at 0915.

Meanwhile, cannon shells from the Zeros' passes shattered the Fortress' forward fuselage. One exploded in the cockpit, badly injuring Zeamer and shattering his leg. It also ruptured hydraulic and oxygen lines causing a fire in the forward fuselage which was soon extinguished. However, the leaking lines presented another immediate problem, for without oxygen at their height the crew would pass out. Zeamer dived the bomber down to 12,000 feet where they could comfortably survive without it.

The shot-up Fortress, with most of the crew injured, limped back to Port Moresby. Nose gunner

/ navigator Lieutenant Joseph Sarnoski died due to blood loss. Zeamer began passing out from blood loss so Staff Sergeant John Able took over the controls under Zeamer's guidance and maintained the Fortress in level flight as it made its way towards Dobodura. In the circuit area co-pilot Lieutenant John Britton, who had been tending the wounds of others, returned to the cockpit to land the bomber. Britton usually always sat forward during the flight, helping explain why he wasn't injured when the instrument panel was damaged by the 20mm rounds exploding behind and below it.

Except for Sarnoski, all the crew survived and Zeamer made a full recovery after long term and extensive medical treatment. Both Zeamer and Sarnoski each were awarded the Medal of Honor: Zeamer for continuing to fly after being critically wounded, and Sarnoski posthumously for continuing to fight after being mortally wounded. The rest of the crew each received the Distinguished Service Cross, making them the most highly decorated aircrew in US military history to this day.

When he returned to Buka, FPO2c Yamamoto Suehiro submitted incorrectly that the Fortress had finally crashed into a Bougainville mountainside, noting that he had personally sighted the wreckage.

While Zeamer's crippled Fortress limped back to Dobodura, back at Buka a total of thirty Zero pilots including all of Warrant Officer O'oki Yoshio's *chutai* who had just landed (minus FPO2c Yahiro Shinichi still being rescued) were hurriedly assembled to be told to depart immediately to Buin. This was a big mission whereby they would join more No. 251 *Ku* Zeros which had flown down from Rabaul that morning to join Zeros from Nos. 582 and 204 *Ku* to escort No. 582 *Ku* Val dive-bombers. The No. 251 *Ku* Zeros were structured into four *chutai* in which O'oki was placed as a *shotaicho*.

The detailed report of substantive shipping number anchored off Lunga obtained by FCPO Mashita Chozo's Irving offered a lucrative target. The combined formations flew down The Slot to bomb the shipping there, however the Americans were well-warned in advance, and launched about a hundred Thirteenth Air Force, USN and US Marine Corps fighters to counter the attack. The mission was a disaster for the Japanese, losing a total of fourteen Zeros and thirteen Vals to the defending US fighters and AA fire. Three of the fourteen Zero pilots lost had been participants in the Fortress mission that morning: Warrant Officer O'oki Yoshio, FPO2c Yamamoto Suehiro and FPO2c Iwano Hiroshi.

Meanwhile, Zeamer's surviving Fortress was again reassigned back to the 8th PRS. The extra armament that Zeamer's crew had added was removed as it was considered too heavy. After serving a few months with the 8th PRS, it was reassigned one last time to the 63rd Bombardment Squadron, which flew only two missions in the bomber, both in late September 1943. It was returned to the US in March 1944 where it was assigned to the Air Technical Service command at Spokane Army Airfield. In July 1944 it was reassigned to the Combat Crew Training Station at Walla Walla Army Air Base, where training was in the process of transitioning to the longer-range B-24. As a result, the obsolete Fortress was transferred after just three weeks service to the Southeast Training Center at Hendricks Field in Florida. There it spent its final days as a

A picture taken of Zeamer's crew around April 1943 shortly after they were transferred to the 65th BS. Medal of Honor awardees Zeamer (left) and Sarnoski (right) are circled.

Lucy in flight a few weeks before its most fateful mission. The B-17E was subsequently repaired and put back into service.

four-engine conversion trainer for first-time bomber pilots. In August 1945, it was flown to Albuquerque, among the first of over fifteen hundred obsolete wartime aircraft to be sold as scrap metal to the Reconstruction Finance Corporation. In fact, the Fortress had come full circle, as the 19th Bomb Group in which the Fortress had first served had been the first Bomb Group stationed at nearby Albuquerque Army Air Field when first activated in 1941. Zeamer died in a nursing home in 2007 at the age of 88, becoming the longest-surviving Medal of Honor recipient from the US Army Air Force.

Jay Zeamer being awarded the Medal of Honour at the Pentagon on 16 January 1944. Chief of the Army Air Forces General "Hap" Arnold is on the far right while his parents look on.

Buka airfield and facilities in June 1943.

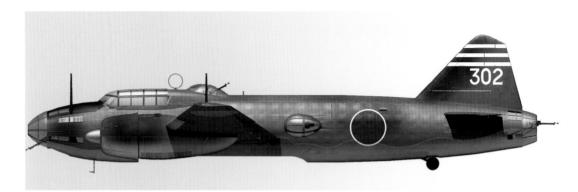

Mitsubishi G4M1 Model 22 tail code 302, No. 702 Ku, ditched 17 June 1943, pilot FCPO Yokokawa Shigeo 横川成男.

Yokokawa's Betty in Port Moresby's spotlights.

CHAPTER 11
Moresby's Final Raid

By mid-1943 the once-powerful IJN bomber force at Rabaul had been reduced to a shadow of its former self. An offensive against Port Moresby consisted of a series of ineffectual night raids which battled weather as much as the enemy. POWs captured from a Betty downed during the very final raid give a valuable insight into these operations.

Anti-aircraft guns could be just as much a powerful adversary as enemy fighters. By mid-1943 Port Moresby hosted a powerful multitude of AA batteries which on the evening of 17 June 1943 fired a total of 1,262 rounds against a pair of loitering Bettys. Aside from the Australian 32nd Heavy Anti-Aircraft Battery, also present were batteries of the US 101st Coast Artillery Battalion. Due to the amount of ordnance fired it will never be ascertained whose guns brought down the victim, a No. 702 *Ku* Betty. The bomber later ditched and the unit log along with three separate crew interrogations give us an intimate glimpse into the last IJN bombing mission against Port Moresby.

At Vunakanau Lieutenant Takahama Haruo planned and conducted the very last two IJN air raids against Port Moresby. These were piecemeal affairs, caused almost no damage, and were both conducted at night. Their curious format epitomises the declining fortunes of a once-powerful air force and underlines the limitations of Pacific night operations. This last hurrah was truly a far cry from the opening days of Port Moresby's air war where Zeros had contested every Allied move alongside substantive Betty formations which regularly appeared overhead.

The air group involved in the last series of raids against Port Moresby was No. 702 *Ku*, a re-invented unit which arose from the remnants of No. 4 *Ku*, which had been one of the very first IJN air units at Rabaul from early 1942. This latter unit had sustained the heaviest losses of any land-attack unit in the IJN. Disbanded at the end of September 1942, its survivors had been sent back to Japan to form the nucleus of No. 702 *Ku*. Lieutenant Takahama had been in charge of a flight of ten Bettys among the nucleus of 49 which left Kisarazu on 1 May 1943. They made their way to Rabaul via Tinian and Truk, although it was inauspicious that two aircraft were lost in transit, with one crew being rescued.

Once they arrived at Rabaul No. 702 *Ku* rejuvenated the theatre's land-attacker objectives. Its commander *hikocho* Kuno Shujo had previously served as *hikocho* for Kisarazu *Ku* and since held other senior staff positions. He authorised a series of nuisance night-time raids against No. 4 *Ku*'s original nemesis, Port Moresby. The first raid underlined the challenge of negotiating New Guinea's mountainous terrain and tropical weather. The tactic was to stagger the Bettys' departure about an hour apart, so they would arrive in pairs over the town at different timeframes to drop 60-kilogram bombs. Two pairs set off on this first mission of 13 May, however only one pair got through and their bombs fell wide of the target at 2025.

A 32ⁿᵈ Heavy Anti-Aircraft Battery machine gun emplacement in the foothills near Seven-Mile 'drome.

The range finder (background) and predicator (fire control mechanism, foreground) seen in a 32ⁿᵈ Heavy Anti-Aircraft Battery position overlooking 14-Mile 'drome.

Another four Bettys failed to reach Port Moresby the next night due to bad weather. The second pair finally found Gasmata on the way home at 2125, then stooged around in the murk trying to find Vunakanau for nearly three hours before landing safely at 0015. It had been a close call.

Undeterred, three pairs of Bettys again tried for Port Moresby on evening of 15 May, led by Lieutenant Sumida Shinhichi. To give new crews maximum operational exposure, most Bettys in May 1943 carried an extra crew member. Only one pair got through, from which Sumida's Betty disappeared taking all eight crew with it, and no damage was done to the target.

The unit turned its attention to patrols from Ballale for the next week, then on 23 May three pairs of Bettys tried to again bomb Moresby. This time they departed much later, the first flight leaving at 2200 and all although three flights claimed to have bombed the target the raid went unrecorded by the Allies. Dirty weather again played its tricks and during the return FPO1c Arai Hayashi force-landed uninjured at 0630 on New Britain.

Still undeterred, three more pairs set off again during the next evening of 24 May. Staggered an hour apart, the first pair departed Vunakanau at 2202. Only one of these pairs got through to the target zone but caused no damage. However, on the return journey two Bettys force-landed on the New Britain coastline, both bombers becoming losses but their crews survived. Clearly all efforts to damage Port Moresby were being badly impeded by the weather, and so it was decided to wait until it improved.

Port Moresby operations resumed around three weeks later on 13 June, this time the initiative planned and led by *chutaicho* Lieutenant Takahama Haruo. The same deployment formula was followed as used previously. Three pairs of Bettys departed Vunakanau in staggered departures that evening about an hour apart, the first leaving at 1645. All three pairs got through to the target but, again, no damage to the Moresby area was recorded by the Allies.

The next mission unfolded on 17 June and became the final one as, once again, it produced a litany of failure. Three airmen were captured from the mission, providing an intimate glimpse into the parameters of a collapsing Japanese air offensive. *Chutaicho* Lieutenant Takahama authorised the mission at short notice, and briefed the six aircraft commanders, some of whom were pilots, only an hour before take-off. Pilot of tail code #302, FCPO Yokokawa Shigeo (aged 23 and a former store clerk), was briefed by commander FCPO Tanaka Bunkichi (aged 20 and a former farmer) only half an hour before departure. None of #302's other crew were briefed on any part of the mission, including the destination. The Bettys would fly in pairs, the first departing from Vunakanau at 1900, and Takahama took off first. Radio silence was enforced for such missions, so there was no communication between aircraft once airborne. Betty #302 was almost a brand new aircraft, built at Mitsubishi's Number Three Nagoya plant only a few months prior. A captured diary shows it had recently had an engine change at Vunakanau.

The second flight got lost and dropped its bombs in the Dobodura area before heading home in poor weather. They finally found Vunakanau where they landed at 0230. Meanwhile the first and third pairs separately bombed Port Moresby's AA positions at 2150 and 2215 hours (2225 hours according to the Japanese log). Three of the four Bettys which hit Moresby could not get find

A pair of No. 702 Ku Bettys parked at Vunakanau in late 1943.

Vunakanau on the return but finally made Kavieng instead at 0135, however the fourth was missing.

We return to when pilot FCPO Yokokawa Shigeo and the crew of #302 approached Port Moresby airspace at 26,000 feet. As was standard modus operandi, Yokokawa descended the bomber to accelerate for the bombing run. They were picked up by searchlights on the approach and fierce anti-aircraft fire followed. Oil and fuel tanks in the inner port wing were hit, and the port engine shut down shortly thereafter. Yokokawa assessed nonetheless they could make an emergency landing at Lae, and successfully negotiated the mountain ranges before reaching the coast. Here Yokokawa descended to 2,000 feet where the thicker air had more lift. However, once again tropical weather would take its toll. The crippled bomber had insufficient power to skirt around a heavy and turbulent rainstorm in their path. Violent turbulence cost valuable altitude, forcing Yokokawa to ditch in a moderate swell off the coastal village of Buso, about 45 miles south of Lae.

The Betty floated for about four minutes while the crew frantically inflated the dull red survival raft with bellows. Pilot Yokogawa decided he would try it alone and swam immediately for shore. The rest of the crew hauled badly injured engineer FPO2c Matsui Mitsuo into the raft where he soon died from blood loss. The remaining six spent an uncomfortable morning of 18 May huddled in the raft in moderate swell, trying to paddle against a strong current towards the mainland. About midday they were forced to abandon the raft due to air leaks. There followed a group discussion as to how far away the shore might be, with observer FCPO Tanaka Bunkichi estimating the distance as five miles. Each now swam separately for their lives, buoyed by their kapok flight vests, but tried to stay together as a group. It was obvious that co-pilot Leading Aircraftsman Sato Ki'ichi was not a strong swimmer and was struggling to stay afloat before the group was separated by the currents.

By late that afternoon tail gunner FPO2c Tanabe Mitsumasa had lost sight of the others. He swam all night and reached a small island around noon on 19 June. There he slept on the beach where the next morning he met Waist gunner FPO1c Murayama Naganori (aged 22 and a former farmer). The pair spent three more nights on the island, then made a log raft to try for the mainland. It took only a few hours to make the New Guinea coast where they soon met villagers who offered to take them to Salamaua. During the journey they were instead captured by a Papuan infantry patrol and turned over to Australian soldiers on 23 June near the village of Sipoma.

Meanwhile pilot FCPO Yokokawa Shigeo had successfully made the mainland shore after a gruelling swim. He then spent nearly six weeks trying to get to Lae but the terrain and his weakened condition prevented him from making much progress. He was soon reduced to stealing food from local gardens and was finally captured on 12 July, after which he was hospitalised in Australia for nearly two and a half months until 21 September. Of Betty #302's crew therefore, one crewman died at sea from wounds, three were captured and it is presumed the other three drowned at sea.

The drawn-out saga thus marked the last Japanese Navy bombing mission against Port Moresby. The town was bombed only one more time, unsuccessfully at night on evening of 20 September 1943 by JAAF Ki-49 Helen bombers.

Fate of the crew of tail code #302

Pilot FCPO Yokokawa Shigeo (POW) captured 12 July near Buso

Co-pilot Leading Aircraftsman Sato Kiichi (missing presumed drowned)

Observer FCPO Tanaka Bunkichi (missing presumed drowned)

Waist gunner FPO1c Murayama Naganori (POW) captured near Sipoma 23 June

Tail Gunner FPO2c Tanabe Mitsumasa (POW) captured near Sipoma 23 June

Radio / top gunner FPO1c Arai Shigeo (missing presumed drowned)

Engineer FPO2c Matsui Mitsuo (died at sea)

One of the two Bettys which force-landed on the New Britain coastline following the failed raid against Port Moresby which departed on 24 May 1943. Both airframes were lost but their crews survived.

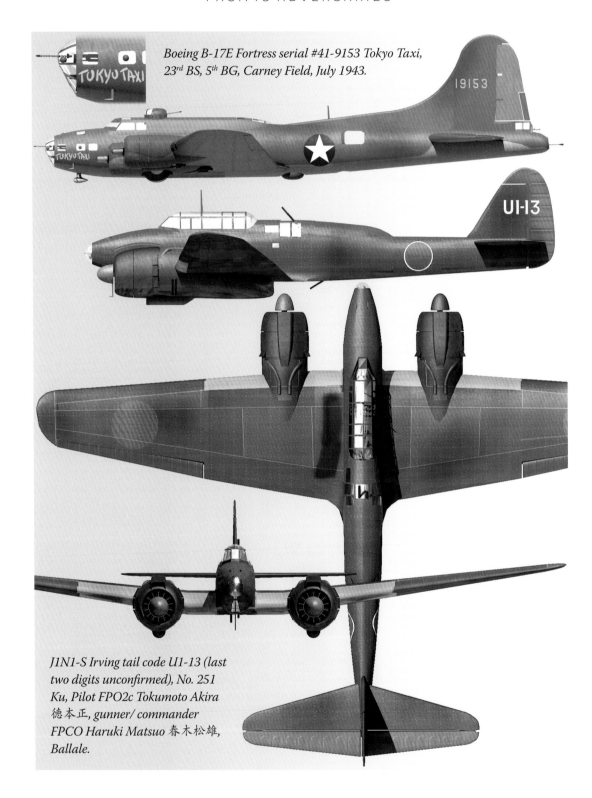

Boeing B-17E Fortress serial #41-9153 Tokyo Taxi, 23rd BS, 5th BG, Carney Field, July 1943.

J1N1-S Irving tail code U1-13 (last two digits unconfirmed), No. 251 Ku, Pilot FPO2c Tokumoto Akira 徳本正, gunner/ commander FPCO Haruki Matsuo 春木松雄, Ballale.

CHAPTER 12
Novel Night Fighter

One of the most peculiar aircraft and weapon combinations in the South Pacific was the use of Irving night fighters with an upwards firing cannon. The novel concept brought success against B-17s, which had otherwise proved exceptionally difficult quarry for Japanese fighter pilots.

The regular but unwelcome night appearance of the Flying Fortress over Rabaul was the catalyst which promoted the concept and then development of the first Japanese night fighter. The new technology was first trialled against Fortresses over Rabaul in mid-May 1943 with No. 251 *Ku* J1N1-S Irving night fighters and soon proved deadly.

Credit for the initiative can be directly traced back to IJN pilot FPO2c Kudo Shigetoshi who had arrived in New Guinea in April 1942 as part of the Tainan *Ku* reconnaissance detachment. Commencing in June, this detachment first conducted familiarisation and training sorties in Mitsubishi C5M2 Babs aircraft from Lae and Rabaul, making their first reconnaissance mission over Horn Island on the northern tip of Australia on 17 June 1942. Then, later that same month several J1N1-C Irving twin-engine land reconnaissance aircraft arrived for trials.

Throughout 1942 Fifth Air Force Fortresses ramped up night raids against the Rabaul area. Such attacks in reality did little physical damage, however these nuisance raids disturbed much needed sleep for those below, and this spurred Japanese retaliation. The Tainan *Ku* Executive officer, Commander Kozono Yasuna, proposed mounting upwards-firing 20mm cannon in the airframe of the J1N1-C Irving, still being trialled for the reconnaissance role. Kudo spurred Kozono on and convinced him that the idea had merit. Kozono flew to Tokyo in November where he robustly promoted the concept. His conception was initially rebuffed by the Department of Navy, however his persistence saw agreement that at least the idea should be tested.

Kozono was meanwhile posted to No. 251 *Ku*, a unit which grew from the reformed Tainan *Ku* sent back to Japan from Rabaul to re-equip and retrain. Two prototype J1N1-S Irving night-fighters were flown to Rabaul via Tinian and Truk for combat testing. In fact, only one reached Rabaul on 10 May 1943, when the other crashed on Tinian following an engine failure. Another replacement was quickly despatched along with two specialists to test the aircraft at Lakunai airfield.

Following these trials, it was the team of Kudo with commander / gunner Lieutenant Sugawara Akira which scored the first Japanese night fighter kill in the South Pacific. They first spotted B-17 *Honikuu Okole* at 0320 on 21 May 1943. Seventeen minutes later they cautiously positioned themselves behind and below the Boeing. When Sugawara opened fire the demise of the Fortress was quick and effective, but Kudo had not finished the morning's work. At 0428 he dispatched another Fortress. Two Fortresses downed on a single mission was unprecedented,

Lieutenant Rex Eckles at the controls of Tokyo Taxi.

particularly given their proven defensive abilities against Japanese fighters.

However, things did not always go as intended. Close-quarter night operations were fraught with danger for both sides and in the early hours of 19 July 1943 the first J1N1-S Irving was lost to combat. Rabaul High Command had decided that No. 251 *Ku* should establish a frontline base at Ballale Island to challenge night bombing operations against Bougainville anchorages and airfields being conducted from Guadalcanal. Accordingly, a detachment of three Irvings was sent to Ballale in early July 1943 where they joined two *chutai* of No. 251 *Ku* Zeros already stationed there. Two Irvings conducted No. 251 *Ku*'s first night patrol from Ballale on 17 July, both departing at 2125 and returning about two and a half hours later with nil results. Pilot FPO2c Tokumoto Akira with observer / gunner FPCO Haruki Matsuo were teamed up to participate in this inaugural mission. In the early hours of the next morning all three Irvings conduced another mission in which Tokumoto's team was again a participant, but again with nil sightings. In the early morning of 19 July at 0040 Tokumoto and Haruki again departed Ballale to patrol southern Bougainville skies. The evening was clear, with about 40% cloud coverage between 10,000 to 12,000 feet.

At 0115 they sighted a "B-24" and made three passes, claiming it shot down, however this is not the case. There were no Liberators airborne that evening and it appears they made a pass against a solitary B-17 making a weather reconnaissance for a nine-bomber raid about

to follow. The attack was not specifically reported by this American crew as they doubtless confused the tracers as being AA fire.

Executive officer of No. 251 Ku, Commander Kozono Yasuna at Lakunai (holding sword). Irving pilot FPO2c Kudo Shigetoshi is standing behind wearing a flying helmet. The seated flight officer on the left is Lieutenant Sugawara Akira. The staff officer wearing glasses is unidentified.

Then, at 0215 Tokumoto and Haruki made three attacks against another B-17, claiming it shot down. When the Fortress was hit it exploded and shrapnel from the blast damaged both of the Irving's engines. Tokumoto was forced to ditch off southern Bougainville where his Irving sank quickly, taking Haruki with it. Tokumoto made it to shore in the aircraft's life raft and was returned to Ballale later that morning. Shortly thereafter he was sent back to Rabaul for several weeks leave. Before he left, he reported that he estimated his Irving had fired 120 rounds to bring down both claimed bombers.

The lost Fortress was B-17E *Tokyo Taxi*, one of nine 5th Bombardment Group Fortresses which had departed Carney Field on Guadalcanal around midnight to bomb Kahili airfield at Buin. *Tokyo Taxi* flown by Lieutenant Rex Eckles led the bomb run from 14,000 feet where it was illuminated by searchlights which at first appeared to converge on *Toyko Taxi*. They then shifted to illuminate *L'il Nell*. Captain Anthony Lucas who was flying *Li'l Nell* then saw tracers from Tokomoto's night fighter above him streak into *Tokyo Taxi* resulting in an immense explosion about ten miles north of Kahili. The other eight Fortresses all returned safely to Carney Field by 0600. When *Tokyo Taxi's* maximum endurance expired at 0900, and despite Lucas' report that it had been brought down, two Fortresses were despatched at 1015 to search for the missing bomber.

Another of the nine Fortresses airborne on evening of 18/19 July 1943 was Boomerang.

Rex Eckles' family had moved to Santa Barbara, California, during the 1930s. At 22 years of age when shot down, Rex had joined the USAAF officer training cadet program at Santa Barbara High School where he had won a saber award for close order drill. He graduated in 1937 then enrolled at the University of California to study agriculture. Later he had enlisted and graduated from flight class 42E. Just prior to shipping out from San Francisco he had married Mary Jane Boggs, who he had first met in Santa Barbara. Lucas returned Eckles' possessions to Mary back in the US when Lucas finished his tour.

Bulky 1,000-pound anti-shipping bombs ready to be loaded from the side of Carney Field, Guadalcanal, for another mission to Kahili.

Douglas C-47A serial #42-23711, 64th TCS, 403rd TCG, Espiritu Santo, September 1943.

The wreckage of the C-47 as it lies today in the jungle of Espiritu Santo. The red-surround star-and-bar is still barely visible.

CHAPTER 13
The White Mug

Tragic aircraft accidents were virtually a daily occurrence at the height of the war in the South Pacific. One example has been remembered by a native village through generations by way of a simple wartime memento.

As occurred too often in the Pacific theatre, often the deadliest adversary was capricious weather rather than the enemy. By September 1943 Guadalcanal hosted several bustling airfields, including two exclusively for fighters, Fighter #1 and Fighter #2. The busiest air route was to Espiritu Santo which saw a mixture of cargo flights, staging runs and aircraft deliveries. On 5 September 1943 a C-47A transport assigned to the 64th Troop Carrier Squadron headed off for another return flight to Santo from Fighter #2 around 1130. Exemplifying interservice co-operation, the USAAF squadron had been busy the past month delivering logistical supplies to USMC Corsair squadrons based at Fighter #2. The C-47A's last radio contact was a routine position report relayed via another C-47 two hours later. This placed it about 270 miles southeast of departure, on track for Turtle Bay airfield on Espiritu Santo.

The transport, flown by Lieutenant Robert Healy, had a crew of five and was almost brand new. Delivered to the USAAF only three months previously, it was the first C-47 delivered to the 64th TCS and was flown to Australia by the current crew. Built at Santa Monica in California it sported a "star and bar" insignia, unusually with red surround. The red piping did not last long in theatre, as most were painted over by the end of 1943 as the colour red too closely resembled a Japanese marking. Nonetheless, Healy's transport still retained the red surround as it continued towards Turtle Bay in scattered to broken cloud with seven miles visibility. Healy's transport was due to arrive at Turtle Bay by late afternoon, around 1630, but failed to do so.

The next morning four of the squadron's C-47s searched all immediate islands and the ocean around the big island of Espiritu Santo for the missing transport in marginal conditions. The cloud ceiling was down to between 400 to 1,000 feet between squalls of heavy rain. Scheduled flights to Guadalcanal branched out to search the area 35 miles either side of track in case the C-47 had ditched. Several B-24s and a USN PBY joined in but to no avail.

Meanwhile at a village at the base of Mount Turi, some fifteen miles northwest of Turtle Bay, a village chief by the name of Kelef Sar gathered a search party to try and locate a large aircraft they were sure they had heard crash in the previous afternoon's rainy weather. Two days later Kelef Sar and his villagers found the intact carcass of Healy's C-47A sprawled in the jungle, with the forward section badly stoved in. One crewmember had survived, navigator Lieutenant Leonard Richardson, who had been sitting behind the cockpit bulkhead at time of impact. Richardson suffered extensive injuries including broken limbs and head injuries. Kelef Sar made his way as quickly as possible to the nearest American airfield where he told the Americans what he had found. A rescue party set out immediately with a tarpaulin stretcher and carried Richardson to the nearest medical facility, Base Hospital #3.

It is clear from the layout and location of the wreck that the pilots let down on approach in cloud and marginal visibility on track for Turtle Bay. Charts at that time were not accurate, especially spot heights, and the C-47 drove cleanly into a gentle slope of Mount Turi at a descent speed of around 170 knots. There was no fire, largely as the aircraft was almost out of fuel.

When sufficiently recovered Richardson returned to the village and presented Kelef Sar with a white mug as a small token of gratitude for saving his life. The mug has been passed down through the generations and the current chief of the village still proudly has it today.

Post-war Richardson married a nurse with whom he had two children. When they had grown up, they returned to the village with their own children where they mounted a bronze plaque outside the village communal hall. It was their way of thanking the villagers for rescuing their father and honouring the four airmen who perished in the crash so many years ago.

Texas Tramp was also assigned to 64th TCS, seen here following a landing accident on Espiritu Santo.

The white coral base runway is evident as this 403rd TCG C-47 is serviced at Pekoa, Espiritu Santo.

A C-47 departs Turtle bay airfield, Espiritu Santo, in late 1943.

*Mitsubishi A6M2 Zero Model 21 tail code 53-160, No. 253 Ku, Tobera,
12 October 1943.*

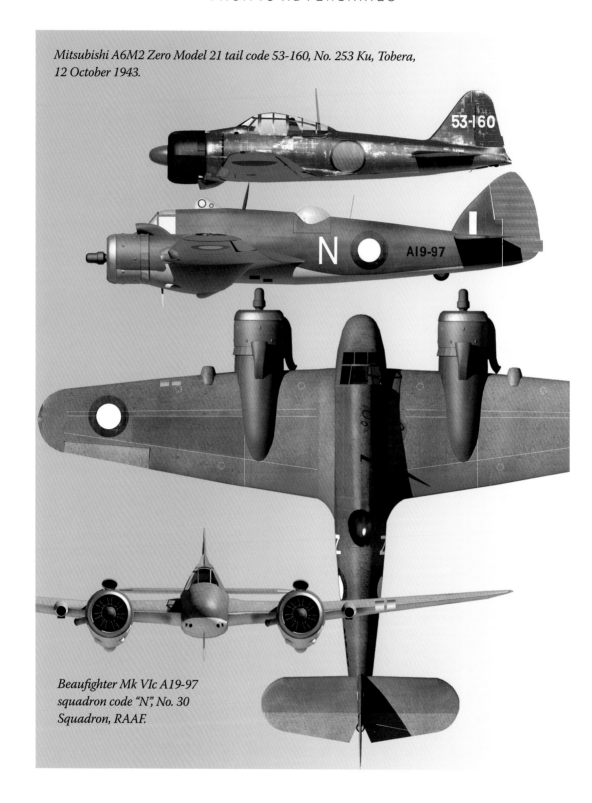

*Beaufighter Mk VIc A19-97
squadron code "N", No. 30
Squadron, RAAF.*

CHAPTER 14
Beaufighter Surprise

During a large Allied raid against Rabaul's airfields in October 1943, circumstances meant a dozen RAAF Beaufighters went in separately after the main force of USAAF B-25 Mitchell strafers escorted by Lightning fighters. The speeding Beaufighters blustered straight into a circuit of Zeros, resulting in a keenly fought low-level engagement.

There is no doubt that the first major low level attack against Rabaul of 12 October 1943 was the one which did the most damage in the Fifth Air Force Rabaul campaign. The strike was a two-punch affair – the first at low level hit the airfields whilst the second would follow about an hour later, a high-altitude attack conducted by Liberators. It was the strafers which took the Japanese completely by surprise at Vunakanau and Rapopo, but Japanese fighters were quick to stir at Tobera. Three pairs of No. 253 *Ku* Zeros had been assigned to patrol Rabaul's skies throughout the day, the first shift departing at 0825. These patrols varied in length of between one to two hours, and the first was joined by a separate *shotai* of three Zeros which launched ten minutes later. Whilst the *shotai* pairs would range further afield and at medium altitudes, the trio led by Lieutenant Hayashi Yoshishige patrolled more closely as to quickly defend against intruders if required. The Japanese were not taking any chances as Rabaul was at that time packed full of aerial reinforcements to bolster their air campaign. The patrolling Zeros at medium altitudes were expecting any trouble to arrive at a similar height. The problem was that the first large scale attack was wholly at low-level. As such, the incoming attackers were more difficult to see, and took Rabaul's fighters by complete surprise.

Although the main strike force against Rabaul's various airfields was overwhelmingly American, a dozen No. 30 Squadron, RAAF, Beaufighters led by Squadron Leader William "Bill" Boulton would specifically target Tobera. The Beaufighters had staged through Dobodura from Wards 'drome near Port Moresby the night before. On the morning of the strike their departure was delayed by dust raised by departing participant USAAF Mitchells. Because of this they took off later than intended at 0815 and arrived late at the fighter rendezvous. Nonetheless, Boulton elected to continue with his squadron alone.

Around 1050, after the Mitchells had completed their strafing runs and the rest of the USAAF squadrons had attacked Rabaul, the Beaufighters were approaching the target area at sea level when they flew towards three oncoming squadrons of 3rd BG strafer B-25s. These totalled 41 Mitchells from the 8th, 13th and 90th Bombardment Squadrons led by Colonel Donald Hall, returning from their strike against Rapopo. The Mitchells, thinking the Beaufighters were enemy Sally aircraft, spread out their formation and fired at the Beaufighters. Fortunately, none were hit. Then a gaggle of Lightnings flying escort above the Mitchells positioned themselves to attack the Beaufighters. Boulton stopped matters getting out of hand with a hasty and robust radio transmission.

3rd Bombardment Group, Rapopo Mission, 12 October 1943.

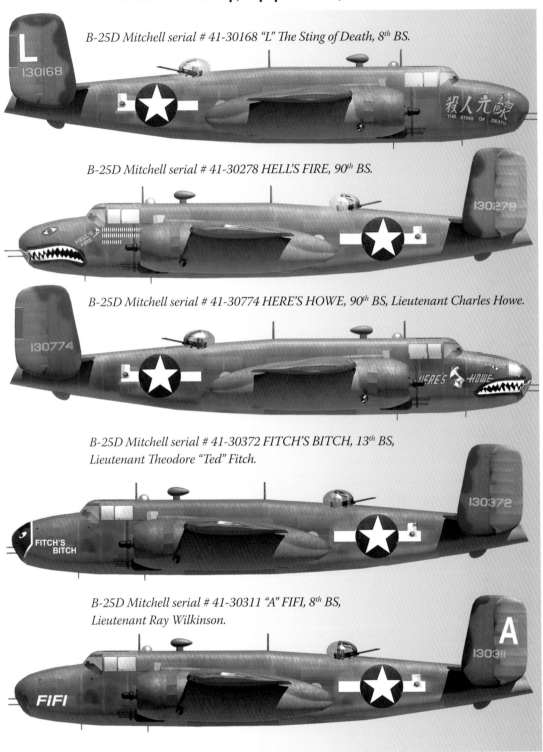

B-25D Mitchell serial # 41-30168 "L" The Sting of Death, 8th BS.

B-25D Mitchell serial # 41-30278 HELL'S FIRE, 90th BS.

B-25D Mitchell serial # 41-30774 HERE'S HOWE, 90th BS, Lieutenant Charles Howe.

B-25D Mitchell serial # 41-30372 FITCH'S BITCH, 13th BS, Lieutenant Theodore "Ted" Fitch.

B-25D Mitchell serial # 41-30311 "A" FIFI, 8th BS, Lieutenant Ray Wilkinson.

The Mitchells' keenness to open fire was understandable. When they had previously passed over Rapopo, six JAAF 14th Sentai Ki-21 Sally bombers had set out for Alexishafen. The first four departed safely however the No. 2 *chutaicho*, Captain Lieutenant Kurano Teruo, had just taken off when the frontal firepower from Hall's Mitchells tore off his wing, killing the entire crew. The sixth Sally was piloted by Lieutenant Yasuda Norito, who aborted the departure and saved his crew. Another six Sallys parked at Rapopo were destroyed by the strafing. In this way the Mitchell crews were primed to assume that the approaching Beaufighters were more Sallys.

We now return to the Beaufighters who blustered into Tobera's circuit area where they unexpectedly encountered eighteen No. 253 *Ku* Zeros. These forewarned Zeros were structured in *shotai* of three and four-aircraft and several were retracting undercarriages when the Beaufighters attacked. The defending Zeros were led by the aggressive Lieutenant Oshibuchi Takashi who had previously served as a division officer with No. 251 *Ku* until it had been recently disbanded. Anti-aircraft fire was sporadic because the Japanese gunners feared hitting their own aircraft. As they stumbled through the Zeros the Beaufighter pilots could see destroyed and burning aircraft at Rapopo, and in the distance huge fires at Vunakanau from the Mitchells' low-level attacks.

The Beaufighters wheeled starboard as they pulled off target, trying to maintain formation and avoiding dogfights. Wing Commander Emerton flying A19-142 fired at one of the Zeros as he approached Rapopo, sweeping over the airfield very low at full power. Three fighters closed on him making rear attacks for five minutes, but he broke away with his ASI reading 280 miles an hour. These were doubtless Lieutenant Hayashi Yoshishige's trio who reported engaging an "A-20A" (no A-20s were present, apparently confused for a Beaufighter) and B-25s at 1105. After more pursuits they returned to Tobera at 1230.

Meanwhile a running fight ensued lasting thirty minutes as the Beaufighters sped away pursued by Zeros. Beaufighter A19-97 was flying close to Emerton's A19-142 as the pair raced for safety. Flown by Flying Officer Robert Stone with navigator Flying Officer Edward Morris-Hadwell, A19-97 was last seen being pursued by Hayashi's trio, and climbing sharply. Beaufighter A19-97 never returned; its wreckage not discovered until 1999. It was determined during the recovery of remains that Japanese forces had visited the crash site and buried the crew nearby. The Beaufighter crashed near the village of Ganai, 30 miles southeast of Rabaul. Oshibuchi lost one of his pilots during a fight with B-25s and P-38s and had two more Zeros badly damaged by gunfire. The seventeen survivor Zeros from this fierce gunfight returned to Tobera at 1145 where they quickly refuelled in anticipation of more attacks. These soon arrived in the shape of high-altitude Liberators.

Meanwhile, the RAAF base at Kiriwina, the closest Allied airfield to Rabaul, became a scene of feverish activity. It was necessary for the American Lightnings to refuel there on the return journey. RAAF ground crews refuelled a continuous stream of these staging aircraft from lunchtime onwards, while overhead squadrons of Liberators, Mitchells and Fortresses passed over continuously. Between 1200 and 1500 fighters from Nos. 76, 77 and 79 Squadrons, RAAF, patrolled Kiriwina's skies but the Japanese sent no raiders to the area. Boulton's eleven surviving

Beaufighters also refuelled at Kiriwina on the way back but returned to Dobodura for a second Rabaul raid planned for early next morning. An afternoon attempt to photograph the results of the raid was stymied when the tasked USAAF F-4 reconnaissance Lightning was intercepted by two Zeros on approach to Rabaul. The unarmed twin turned back to base. It had been deterred by two of Hayashi's No. 253 *Ku* flyers who, despite the raid, had kept up their patrols throughout the rest of the day. The last Zero patrol landed at Tobera at 1820.

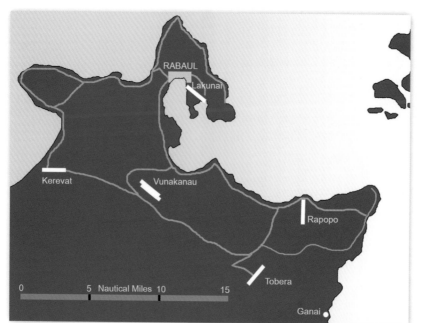

Rabaul's five airfields in late 1943, and the village of Ganai near where Beaufighter A19-97 crashed on 12 October 1943. Kerevat was used only for emergency purposes.

Three 90th BS B-25 pilots who flew the 12 October 1943 Rabaul mission are (left to right) Lieutenant Dick Ellis, Major Jock Henebry and Lieutenant Charles Howe. Ellis flew Seabiscuit, while Henebry led the squadron in Notre Dame de Victoire. The fourth pilot on the far right is Lieutenant "Doc" Gilmour.

Beaufighter A19-97 about to receive a replacement rudder at Wards 'drome on 10 May 1943, about five months before it was lost.

A low-level photo taken of Tobera's concrete taxiway during an October 1943 strike.

Beaufighter A19-142 which was flown by Wing Commander Emerton over Tobera on 12 October 1942.

Model 22 Zero tail code 53-112 of No. 253 Ku aflame over Rabaul in late 1943 as captured on gun camera.

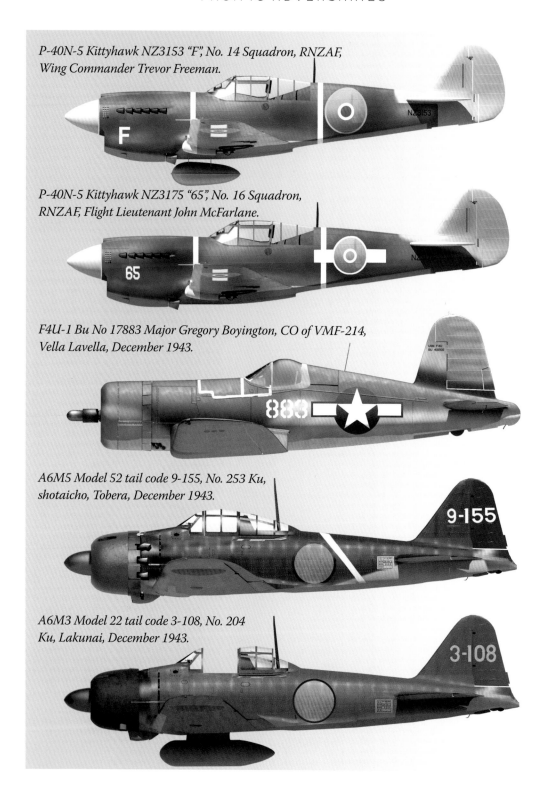

P-40N-5 Kittyhawk NZ3153 "F", No. 14 Squadron, RNZAF, Wing Commander Trevor Freeman.

P-40N-5 Kittyhawk NZ3175 "65", No. 16 Squadron, RNZAF, Flight Lieutenant John McFarlane.

F4U-1 Bu No 17883 Major Gregory Boyington, CO of VMF-214, Vella Lavella, December 1943.

A6M5 Model 52 tail code 9-155, No. 253 Ku, shotaicho, Tobera, December 1943.

A6M3 Model 22 tail code 3-108, No. 204 Ku, Lakunai, December 1943.

CHAPTER 15
Kiwi Wingco Down

Towards the end of 1943 large Allied raids against Rabaul were commonplace and often met swarms of defending Zeros. On 17 December a RNZAF contingent of Kittyhawks arrived over Rabaul alone, and the subsequent engagement resulted in the loss of the commander of the RNZAF Fighter Wing, Wing Commander Trevor Freeman.

Around mid-morning on 17 December 1943 the telephone at the No. 204 *Ku* operations post at Toma near Vunakanau rang. It was a warning from the IJN centre at Rabaul that their outpost at on New Ireland had reported that about two dozen Allied fighters were headed their way. At 1015 seven No. 204 *Ku* Zeros led by Lieutenant Ito Suzuo were airborne and climbed eastwards towards the intruders.

Wing Commander Trevor Freeman was the most senior RNZAF pilot in theatre and was leading the RNZAF's first major offensive air operation, which was about to receive the attention of Ito's flyers. From the city of Dunedin on New Zealand's South Island, Freeman had previously served in the European theatre with the RAF flying both Spitfires and Wellingtons. After completing 58 missions he returned to New Zealand in February 1943 where he was appointed Director of Air Operations. He was now serving as CO of the RNZAF Fighter Wing in the Pacific. On this morning, Freeman led 22 P-40N Kittyhawks from Nos. 14 and 16 Squadrons, RNZAF. Two had dropped out on the way, but shortly behind the Kittyhawks were more substantive formations, comprising 32 Corsairs from US Marine squadrons VMF-214 (led by Major Gregory Boyington), VMF-222, VMF-223 and VMF-216; along with two dozen F6F Hellcats from USN squadrons VF-33 and VF-40.

All units had departed Ondonga and Vella Lavella air bases on New Georgia at dawn that morning and headed for Torokina on Bougainville where they refueled for the mission. By this stage of the war Rabaul had been subjected to major aerial campaigns by both the Fifth and Thirteenth Air Forces, as well as major carrier strikes in mid-November 1943. Despite Allied claims of hundreds of aerial victories during this campaign, this had not been the case, and in fact on the second-biggest strike of 2 November 1943 the Americans had come off a poor second best to the defenders. Rabaul's worn down air defences still hosted three fighter IJN air groups – Nos. 201, 204 and 253 *Ku*. The first two were fighting under an integrated command structure based at Vunakanau, while No. 253 *Ku* was operating independently from Tobera. Following Ito's seven Zeros, two more combined Nos. 201 / 204 *Ku* formations followed. The first of eight launched fifteen minutes later, followed by 39 more at 1040. About ten miles to the southeast at Tobera, an eclectic mix of Model 21, Model 22 and Model 52 Zeros also raised dust, the last of which was airborne at 1055.

The Allied formations had split into two groups when the RNZAF Kittyhawks had proceeded ahead of the Americans without waiting for them at the rendezvous point. Apart from the

A pair of RNZAF No. 16 Squadron P-40N-5 Kittyhawks at Vella Lavella, parked in front of a Corsair.

unplanned separate formations, the rest of the mission was proceeding to plan; the Kittyhawks would patrol the lower altitudes between 10,000 to 15,000 feet, the USN F6F Hellcats at medium altitudes between 15,000 to 20,000 feet, while the Marine Corsairs would patrol higher at 20,000 to 26,000 feet.

From their high but distant vantage point, many Corsair pilots witnessed Ito's seven Zeros fall into the Kittyhawks ahead of them just west of Hunter Point on New Ireland. From the furious combat which followed, Freeman flying NZ3153 and Flight Lieutenant John McFarlane flying NZ3175 were both shot down. Freeman, last seen being pursued by four Zeros, likely hit the water near Hunter Point but no-one was quite sure. The Japanese combat logs are detailed, however many of the claims were for "P-39s" a confused (but common) misidentification for other types as no Airacobras were present. With so many Japanese claims made it is difficult to be sure which Zero pilot shot down Freeman, however a likely contender is Superior Airman Nagano Michihiko flying on the far right of Ito's four-man *shotai*, the first Japanese to engage that morning. McFarlane later went down somewhere near Praed Point after the Kittyhawks fought further battles with the many other Zeros which arrived on the scene.

The staggered Allied formations of Corsairs and Hellcats also fell into the Zeros with the American pilots having a range of experiences from no contact to intense combat. Commander John Remberts and his VF-40 Hellcats saw no combat, while the VMF-214 Corsairs became embroiled in widespread fighting, mainly with No. 253 *Ku*, which spread widely over Rabaul's skies. From these encounters Lieutenant Bragdon had the narrowest escape when his guns failed strafing Lakunai strip. As he pulled away and headed westwards towards Tobera he was jumped by six "Tonys" which chased him for 65 miles. Bragdon reported that at least one had diagonal stripes on the upper surfaces of its wings, along with a diagonal on its fuselage. At full power of 50 inches of manifold pressure and 2,700 RPM, Bragdon was barely able to pull ahead of his pursuers. He finally got home with many hits to his airframe. The No. 253 *Ku* Zeros had returned to Tobera by 1140, the only IJN unit to report combat with Corsairs.

When it was over the Allied fighters claimed nine Japanese aircraft: five by the RNZAF Kittyhawks and four between the USN squadrons. In fact there were four successful kills: one No. 958 *Ku* Jake floatplane was shot down by Corsairs as it tried to land at Malaguna Bay, one No. 201 *Ku* pilot bailed out and was rescued, No. 204 *Ku* pilot Superior Airman Haruyama Isamu was missing and No. 253 *Ku* pilot Superior Airman Kato (first name undecipherable) also failed to return, and was likely one of the Corsair claims. Six more Zeros were hit including a No. 253 *Ku* Zero flown by Superior Airman Kawado Kojiro who was wounded.

Despite the intensity of the Rabaul air war, there is an entry in one of the Japanese operational logs from this day which reminds us that minutiae still have its place in war. This is evidenced whereby a superior made a note to his subordinate operations clerk:

> Don't enter the report across both the daily report and victim columns. Write your report of the encounter separately and attach. Do not confuse such matters and exercise more care in future.

Lieutenant Ito Suzuo's seven flyers including Superior Airman Nagano Michihiko, the only one in his two *shotai* who had claimed a fighter, returned to Vunakanau at 1150. Freeman is memorialised today at the Bourail Memorial, which is the New Zealand war cemetery located on New Caledonia's southern shore.

The central IJN communications centre at Rabaul which received and relayed observation post warnings.

RNZAF fighter pilots on Guadalcanal in 1943.

Maintenance crew inspect combat damage to a No. 204 Ku Model 22 Zero at Vunakanau in early 1944.

F6F-3 Hellcats of VF-40 lined up around the time of the mission, which Commander John Rembert led in #10 on far left.

An RNZAF Kittyhawk being towed to its hardstand on Vella Lavella in late 1943.

Mitsubishi A6M5 Model 52 tail 53-104, Warrant Officer Iwamoto Tetsuzo 岩本徹三, Rabaul, late 1943.

Vought F4U-1A Corsair Bu No 55995, VF-17, assigned to Lieutenant (jg) Ira Kepford, Piva Yoke, Bougainville, February 1944.

CHAPTER 16
The Last Rabaul Fighter Commander

During February 1944 the last Zero unit remaining at Rabaul, No. 253 Ku, flew its final defensive mission before withdrawing to Truk in the Central Pacific. Remarkably, the leader of this unit, Lieutenant-Commander Okamoto Harutoshi, had pioneered fighter operations at Rabaul as far back as January 1942.

In late July 1943, the Zero pilots of No. 253 *Ku* left Rabaul for Saipan to re-equip and regroup following a period of regular, fierce combat. They left behind their Zeros which were reassigned to other fighter units in the 26th Air Flotilla. At Saipan on 18 August 1943, Lieutenant-Commander Okamoto Harutoshi was appointed No. 253 *Ku's* new *hikotaicho*.

The importance of Okamoto and his contribution to the Rabaul air war cannot be overstated. He was an original and key architect of the structure and tactics of IJN land-based operations in the Pacific. Okamoto was the first air commander to arrive at Rabaul way back on 26 January 1942 when he led two detachments to Lakunai airfield of Chitose *Ku* A5M4 Claudes, colloquially known as the "Okamoto *Butai*". Shortly thereafter the new Rabaul fighter detachment was amalgamated into No. 4 *Ku* making this *kokutai* a combined fighter / bomber unit. On 28 February 1942 Okamoto led the first Zero strike against Port Moresby when six Zeros strafed the harbour. Okamoto's Zero in this early era was tail code F-115, discernible by its two thin black bands around the fuselage denoting his role as *chutaicho*.

Now in early September 1943, after serving a considerable stint in Japan during which he had been promoted to Lieutenant-Commander, Okamoto returned to Rabaul, this time to Tobera airfield. By now a substantive base with a concrete runway, ground crews had painted Zero silhouettes on the cement parking areas as a decoy. Rather than offensive operations, Okamoto's unit became involved in defending Rabaul, first countering the October / November 1943 Rabaul campaigns by the Fifth Air Force and then later USN carrier strikes. In that timeframe No. 253 *Ku* was also a major participant during Operation Ro-Go. Okamoto remained *hikotaicho* throughout this challenging time, right up until the end of January 1944, when he was replaced by Lieutenant Hirano Tatsuo. Unbeknownst to the Allies, the IJN decided to withdraw all air units from Rabaul in February 1944 and Okamoto's talents would be required for the next stage of the Pacific War. Meanwhile in Japan, and to honour Okamoto's leadership, a patriotic war song was composed titled *Souretsu! Okamoto Butai* (Behold the Heroic Okamoto air unit). The song's words glorified the heroic achievements of No. 253 *Ku* under Okamoto's leadership, the last Zero unit to defend Rabaul.

By the end of January 1944, No. 253 *Ku* was the only fighter unit able to credibly defend Rabaul as the severe attrition rate had worn down all other fighter units. Combinations of USN, Thirteenth Air Force, Fifth Air Force and even RNZAF squadrons had sent over incessant formations which pounded the town and airfields. On a daily basis, weather permitting, a mixture of P-38s, P-40s,

Lieutenant (jg) Ira Kepford with his Corsair #29 at Piva Yoke on 6 March 1944.

F4Us, F6Fs, TBFs, SBDs, B-25s and B-24s contested Rabaul's skies.

The last day of major fighter combat over Rabaul unfolded on 19 February 1944 when 26 No. 253 *Ku* Zeros, about half of which were late Model 52s, took on two dozen USN Corsairs from VF-17 for nearly an hour commencing at 0920. Led by Lieutenant-Commander John Blackburn from Piva Yoke on Bougainville, the Corsairs escorted 48 SBDs from VC-38, VMSB-241 and VB-98. These dive-bombed Lakunai alongside 23 TBFs of VMTB-143, six of which carried rockets. This combined bombing force carried out their task unmolested mostly due to the aggressive VF-17 pilots. The Zeros lost three in combat, then returned to Tobera at 1015 where they refuelled and took off again fifteen minutes later. They scoured Rabaul's skies anticipating further enemy attacks which failed to materialise, returning at 1600. Other Corsair and Hellcat units patrolled at higher altitude that day but met no Zeros. One of the Corsair units was VMF-216 which escorted a dozen Liberators, one of which briefly encountered a Zero which made a half-hearted pass.

It was VF-17 Corsairs which shot down the last Zero pilot over Rabaul, Superior Seaman Yamaguchi Saichi. Two more No. 253 *Ku* pilots went missing during a battle in which both sides made extravagant claims. VF-17 claimed thirteen Zeros against a real score of three. The Japanese outdid the Americans for excess however, claiming one Liberator, seven Corsairs, one Hellcat and two TBFs, a total of eleven. In fact, not one Allied aircraft was lost.

The Corsair pilot who had the narrowest escape of the day was division leader Lieutenant (jg) Ira Kepford. During the approach to Rabaul his wingman turned back due to engine trouble, so Kepford decided to accompany him. Shortly after the turn Kepford spotted a floatplane low on the water and accepted the temptation to strafe it. However, he himself was set upon by a gaggle of Zeros which had broken away from the main Zero force. He fled northwards but was quickly boxed in by three Zeros. Kepford activated his Corsair's water injection, a new experimental feature installed in several of the squadron's fighters, to help him pull ahead, but the device worked fitfully. He then tried to lose them flying low over New Ireland, but without success. Well north of Wakes Island he made a sudden left turn to get home. He saw one of his pursuers crash into the water while attempting to turn inside him.

Following this last big engagement over Rabaul, in the early morning of 20 February the IJN initiated their evacuation plan. Early before sunrise the majority of No. 253 *Ku*'s Zeros prepared

Pilots of the 105th Naval Base Air Unit pose for the camera at Rabaul in January 1945.

to withdraw to Truk. Their 23 remaining serviceable fighters departed Tobera at 0630 for the four-and-a-half-hour ferry flight led by a Betty bomber. Two more followed separately at 1130. Fifteen Zeros undergoing repair were left behind, later rendered airworthy by the 105th Naval Base Air Unit headed by Commander Hori Tomoyoshi.

Vice Admiral Kusaka Junichi, commander of the Eleventh Air Fleet, went out to Tobera to farewell the fighters. The decision to immediately withdraw Rabaul's airpower had been made by Admiral Koga Mineichi, Commander of the Combined Fleet, in response to a series of massive carrier strikes against Truk. Although Koga had assured Kusaka that the Zeros would eventually return to Rabaul, Kusaka felt certain that Tokyo had abandoned Rabaul. The orderly departure of aircraft, pilots, and ground crews to Truk took five days to complete. The Zeros were followed to Truk by six Bettys, eight Vals, ten Judys and six Kates.

Kusaka gave orders to render airworthy the remaining fifteen Zeros left behind if possible. A handful of veteran pilots also stayed on, supplemented by about thirty inexperienced ones, many of whom had remained behind as they were incapacitated. This motley inventory was complemented by one Dinah, four decommissioned No. 151 *Ku* Irving night fighters and a handful of unserviceable Mavis flying boats. Nonetheless, the small No. 253 *Ku* detachment of Zeros did become airworthy, initially fielding patrols and offensive missions of as many as eight fighters until these were whittled down to just a handful of airworthy machines by the time of Rabaul's surrender in September 1945.

We conclude with the fate of Lieutenant-Commander Okamoto Harutoshi, the first and

last commander of Rabaul's Zeros. In early 1944 he survived a ferry flight of thirteen Zeros from Truk to Guam, during which five were shot down by US fighters. The Zeros remaining at Truk were destroyed on the ground after which Okamoto was evacuated to Japan by submarine. Back in Japan he was appointed *buntaicho* of No. 252 *Ku* on 19 November 1944. Okamoto lived a long life post-war during which he wrote his memoirs and served with the Japanese Self-Defence Force.

Lieutenant-Commander Okamoto Harutoshi, the last Rabaul hikotaicho, and key figure in the Rabaul air war.

A Model 22 Zero at Tobera airfield which kept operating throughout 1944.

Comment on Markings

Warrant Officer Iwamoto Tetsuzo became one of the IJN's highest-scoring pilots and was flying as a *shotaicho* in the second *chutai* for both 19 February 1944 missions. As such, it is likely he was among the bunch which harassed Kepford. The No. 253 *Ku* operations log shows that in early 1944 Iwamoto was sharing the unit's inventory with dozens of other pilots. Iwamoto cites the aircraft numbers -102 and -104 from his logbook as the ones he most often flew. Note that Iwamoto's memoirs are not based on diary entries, but rather on three notebooks outlining his exploits, written about a decade after the war. Iwamoto died prematurely in 1955 at 38 years of age from post-surgery complications. His memoirs cite evidence that some of Rabaul's Zeros in late 1943 / early 1944 sported victory markings when he wrote that in January 1944:

> The number of cherry blossom victory markings on my plane increased. From a distance, it looked as though the entire rear fuselage had been re-painted pink . . . the number of victory markings on my fighter soon reached 60, no less than what had been on my previous plane. But, upon inspection by the maintenance crew, it was decided to change the engine, so I had to farewell my 253-102 for a while, and instead fly 253-104.

The prefix 253- was never used by the unit, and Iwamoto is doubtless referring to tail codes 53-102 and 53-104. It is likely both -102 and -104 were either late Model 22s or Model 52s with dark green / brown camouflage. The single oblique stripe is portrayed is it appeared on No. 253 *Ku shotaicho* fighters in late 1943. However, it must be underlined that the profile in this chapter is speculative. It has been portrayed as an early Model 52 without exhaust stubs which fits the timeframe in which Iwamoto was allocated the fighter.

Pilots of No. 253 Ku at Rabaul in January 1944.

Warrant Officer Iwamoto Tetsuzo (circled) with other No. 253 Ku pilots at Tobera in February 1944.

ACKNOWLEDGEMENTS

Research for this volume is drawn only from primary sources. The author's vast private archival collection includes private correspondence amassed over four decades for which it is not practicable to further credit.

Special thanks to a true aficionado, Bernard Baeza for sharing some of his rare Japanese photo collection.

Acknowledgements also to Pacific War Air Historical Associates (PAWHA) members Ed DeKiep, Luca Ruffato (deceased), Osamu Tagaya, and Jim Lansdale (deceased). Thanks to Justin Taylan's encyclopaedic website www.pacificwrecks.com; to Steve Birdsall (Australia) for B-17 snippets. Thanks also to Ryan Toews, Nick Millman, and Bruce Gamble over the years.

Thanks to Haruki Ichiki and Kunio Iwashita, President of Zero Fighter Association, Shinozaki Yoshiharu (deceased), former President of 705 *Ku* veterans Association. Special thanks to Russell Harada in Rabaul for interpreting some esoteric *kanji*, and Ezaki Yumi in Canberra for translation work on Admiral Kusaka Jinichi's diary.

SOURCES – JAPANESE LANGUAGE

Gatto Tesshu Go, Southeastern Area Naval Operations.

Historical Monograph Series - summary of 1943 South Seas operations by Japanese high Command (contained in Southeast Naval Operations part 2 translated by US General Headquarters Far East Command, Military Intelligence Section 1952).

Otaka Nakajima, The Pacific War as Viewed from the Combined Fleet Operations Room.

Hata Ikuhiko (editor), The Imperial Army and Navy Comprehensive Encyclopaedia, University of Tokyo Press.

Tokuki Matsuda, Kakuta Kakuji: The Warrior who Pushes Through the Enemy, PHP Bunko 2009.

Sanwa Tami, Navy Family (author is Rear-Admiral Sanwa Yoshiwa's daughter).

Meiji Centennial Series (Volume 74) History of the Naval Academy Hara Shobo.

Hata & Izawa, IJNAF Fighter Units/Aces (used for guidance).

Intercepted radio message 12 October 1943 Rabaul air raid from Southeastern Force Action Summary.

Yoshida Hajime memoirs "Samurai Zero-sen Kisha" (cameraman for Nichiei).

Interrogation Reports & Memoirs

Interrogation reports for 702 *Ku* pilot FCPO Yokokawa Shigeo, and crewmembers waist gunner FPO1c Murayama Naganori and tail Gunner FPO2c Tanabe Mitsumasa. Interrogations of 582 *Ku* pilot FPO2c Nakagawa Matao, 204 *Ku* pilot Leading Aircraftsman Kato Masao, and other numerous Betty crew members.

Memoirs of No. 2 *Ku* Zero pilot WO Tsunoda Kazuo, Commander Okumiya, staff officer to Rear Admiral Kakuta Kakuji and 204 *Ku buntaicho*, Lieutenant Kofukuda Mitsugu.

Diary of Vice-Admiral Ugaki Matome, Chief of Staff of the Combined Fleet.

Diary of Vice Admiral Kusaka Jinichi.

Tabulated Records of Movement

Hitachi Maru, Kisaragi Maru, Toyu Maru, Nissan Maru No.3, Hibari Maru and *Nojima Maru.*

Kodochosho (unit operational logs)

Fighter units Chitose *Ku*, Tainan *Ku*, 3 *Ku*, 201 *Ku*, 204 *Ku*, 251 *Ku*, 253 *Ku*, and 582 *Ku*. Bomber units Kisarazu *Ku*, Takao *Ku*, Misawa *Ku*, Genzan *Ku*, 1 *Ku*, 4 *Ku*, 702 *Ku*, 751 *Ku* and 705 *Ku*. Floatplane units 802 *Ku* and 851 *Ku*.

SOURCES – ALLIED

USN ships logs for USS *Chicago*, USS *Celeno* (AK-76), USS *Strong* (DD467).

Relevant official USAAF unit histories via Maxwell AFB (microfilm), including but not limited to 38th Bombardment Group (including Sunsetters Magazine, numerous editions), USAAF squadron records for 68th, 70th, 339th, 8th PRS, 403rd BS and 64th TCS.

Diary of Captain Anthony Dean Lucas July 19, 1943 who was pilot of B-17E "Li'll Nell" 41-9222.

Come What Will, Richard W. Titus, recollections of 101st AAA.

USN official records for VMF-124, VMF-215, VMF-211, VMF-214, VMF-221, VMF-212, VMF-213, VMF-225, VMF-223, VF-17, VPB-101, VF-11, VF-10 and VF-17.

Statement by 35th Infantry officer, Guadalcanal, Captain F.P. Mueller.

Memoirs of Joe Hewitt, CO of RAAF No. 9 Operational Group contained in 'Adversity in Success'.

RAAF Field Intelligence, RNZAF and USAAF combat reports filed in Australian Archives, numerous but including from series A9695 and A9696, and operational logs of RAAF Nos. 30, 75, 76 and 77 Squadrons, RNZAF unit logs for 14 and 16 Squadrons.

Australian War Memorial files, including AWM 66/ 433, AWM 64/1/44, AWM 54 812/3/10, AWM 54 963/22/20.

Port Moresby radar logs May/ June/ July 1943.

Logs for Australian 32nd Heavy Anti-Aircraft Battery (AIF) and US 101st Anti-aircraft Battery.

Private correspondence of RAAF aircrew as archived in AWM PRO holdings.

Numerous RAAF Squadron combat reports and ATIS intelligence reports (numerous).

Keith Rundle RAAF patrol reports 1962 Bogia/ Madang region.

Diary John Florence of 6th NFS.

CILHI crash site reports 1964 - 1993.